KINDNESS HEROES

Ordinary People Doing Extraordinary Things

JACKIE KURTZ

First published in 2025.
Printed in the United States of America.

ISBN: 979-8-9945253-0-2

INTRODUCTION
HOW ONE LIFE SPARKED A MOVEMENT OF KINDNESS

This book began with a single ripple.

Matt Kurtz was a person who quietly and consistently chose kindness, not for recognition, not for praise, but because he believed in doing good for good's own sake. He helped others without hesitation, lifted spirits with humor and compassion, and made people feel seen and valued.

When Matt lost his battle with mental illness at the age of 32, we were left with deep grief and one guiding question: *How can we honor Matt in a way that reflects the legacy he left behind?* We decided the best way to honor him was to keep his ripple of kindness going. So, we created **Matt's Kindness Ripples On**, (MKRO) a small nonprofit with one big mission: to shine a light on kind people and spread kindness in his name. We give Kindness Awards to those who inspire others through their everyday acts of kindness, and Kindness Grants to support people bringing their kindness projects to life.

What began as a tribute to one beautiful life has grown into a community of kindness heroes. Every person in this book has received either a Kindness Grant or a Kindness Award from Matt's Kindness Ripples On. Every grant and award recipient is proof that goodness is not only alive but thriving. These are the people who plant seeds of hope in dark soil. Who use what little they have to give others more. Who turn their own pain into purpose, and their compassion into action.

This book is a celebration of them.

You'll meet a nurse who turned yarn into magic by creating whimsical wigs for children battling cancer. A man in recovery who created a nonprofit that provides foster care for pets while their owners undergo addiction treatment. A couple who built free food pantries in low-income neighborhoods. A teacher who saw a quiet need and launched a book revolution, getting thousands of stories into the hands of kids who had none. And a high school student who turned a personal loss into a movement of empathy.

This book is a collection of their stories. None of them asked to be featured. None of them did it for applause. They simply saw a need, and met it with open hearts and outstretched hands.

Between each story, you'll find a quote about kindness, little reminders that even on our most difficult days, we have the power to make the world a better place. These words are here to lift you, to challenge you, and to gently nudge you into action.

Kindness Heroes is not just a book of good deeds. It's a map of what's possible when people choose generosity over apathy. It's a record of Matt's legacy living on in the actions of strangers who may never have met him, but who embody his spirit all the same.

Our hope is that these stories move you, inspire you, and stay with you long after you turn the final page. But even more than that, we hope they stir something inside you, a reminder that you, too, are capable of incredible kindness. That you don't have to be rich, famous, or perfect to make a difference. You just have to begin.

Kindness isn't a grand gesture. It's a ripple. And every ripple starts with one brave, generous act.

And at the end of this book, we return to Matt, not in grief, but in gratitude, to honor the life that sparked it all.

Thank you for reading. Thank you for believing in kindness. And thank you, truly, for being part of Matt's ripple.

— Jackie, Ron, and Brian Kurtz
(Matt's mom, dad, and brother)

Matt Kurtz 1985-2017

TO MY BOYS:

Matt - I miss you every day.

Brian - There's nothing I've loved more than being your mom (and Matt's). You captured my heart the moment you were born.

Ron - None of this would've been possible without you. Thank you for always being there, and for your endless love and support.

CONTENTS

Introduction How One Life Sparked a Movement of Kindness ... 3

1. Weaving Joy ... 10

2. Second Chances ... 14

3. A Sanctuary Built by Love ... 18

4. The Everlasting Hug ... 22

5. From Waste to Hope ... 26

6. Serving Second Chances ... 30

7. Changing Young Lives ... 34

8. A Chapter of Kindness ... 38

9. Filling the Gap ... 42

10. Serving Hope ... 46

11. From ER to Empowerment ... 50

12. Catio Magic ... 54

13. Where Kindness Begins ... 58

14. Shopping Angels ... 62

15. Coloring Outside the Lines ... 66

16. From Wine Night to Wetlands ... 70

17. Beauty with Purpose ... 74

18. From Patient to Provider ... 78

19. Spreading Literacy and Joy ... 82

20. Kindness in Motion ... 86

21. Baking a Better World .. .. .90

22. Embracing Identity. 94

23. From Wall Street to the Ocean Floor . .. .98

24. Casting Hope 102

25. A Voice for the Planet 106

26. From Hunger to Hope.. 110

27. Eighteen Acts, Endless Impact.. 114

28. And Then Came the Ripples.. 117

29. The Road to Kindness 122

30. From Isolation to Inclusion. 127

31. What's Your 50? 131

32. Taking Ownership.. 135

33. When Kindness Fights Back 139

34. Hope Takes the Field . .. .143

35. The Kindness Ambassador 147

36. A Life of Kindness 151

37. Kindness, Lived Daily 155

38. Bridging Borders with Compassion. 160

39. A Bundle of Compassion . .. .164

40. Sidewalks of Hope.. 168

41. Sheltering with Compassion 172

42. Turning Pages, Changing Lives. 176

43. The Power of Small Wishes. 180

44. Warm Hands, Warm Hearts 184

45. Changing Minds Through Music. 188

46. Serving Kindness, One Meal at a Time 192

47. Wheels of Joy. .. … 196

48. Restoring Women's Voices 200

49. Kindness in Every Basket. 204

50. Creating Belonging Through Soccer 208

51. Spreading Smiles One Episode at a Time . .. .212

52. Planting Hope .. … 216

53. Hearts of Kindness.. .. … 220

54. Champions for Seniors . .. … 224

55. Carrying Love, Not Trash Bags .. .. … 228

56. Fighting for Their Future. 232

57. The Mad Hatter Project .. … 236

58. Leading with Heart. .. … 240

59. A Life Woven with Kindness and Purpose 244

60. Light In Dark Places.. 248

61. Widening Horizons 252

62. Matt Kurtz: A Life of Quiet Kindness 256

Keep the Kindness Going .. .. .260

Meet the Kindness Heroes .. .. .262

About the Author .. .. .272

Acknowledgements .. .. .274

WEAVING JOY

olly Christensen didn't set out to change the world. She just wanted to bring a little light to one little girl's life.

In 2014, a close friend's daughter was diagnosed with cancer. Holly, an oncology nurse, knew the grueling road ahead: endless hospital visits, medications, and the inevitable hair loss that often steals more than hair. It takes away a child's sense of self. One night, staring at a basket of yarn, Holly had a spark of genius. She pulled out soft strands of golden yarn and began to weave. Hours later, she held a Rapunzel wig in her hands, bright and playful, the kind of thing that could make a child forget for a moment what she was fighting.

When the little girl slipped the wig on, the room shifted. She spun in circles, her braid flying, laughter spilling out like magic had snuck in through the door. For that moment, she wasn't a patient tethered to tubes and treatments. She was a princess again. Holly watched through tears, realizing she hadn't just made a wig. She had given back a piece of childhood.

Her friend asked the question that would change every-thing: *"How many other kids could feel this joy?"*

Boom, The Magic Yarn Project was born.

At first, Holly thought she'd make a few more wigs. She posted a casual call for yarn donations online, expecting a handful of responses. Instead, her inbox flooded. Strangers she had never met, teachers, crafters, parents, even hospital work-ers, all chimed in to say, *"How can I help?"*

Soon, Holly's one-car garage turned into a buzzing workshop. Yarn piled high against the walls, scissors clicked in every corner, and her three kids jumped in too, cutting and winding strands.

"It's been so rewarding to see my children learn to reach be-yond themselves," Holly said. "When they see the faces of the kids who receive these wigs, it sparks compassion that will stay with them forever."

The movement spread like wildfire. Schools, churches, and community centers began hosting wig-making workshops. Incarcerated women crocheted beanies for the wigs, grateful to send comfort beyond prison walls. In Seattle, a Seahawks player showed up to make an Elsa wig for a young fan. From grandmothers to teenagers, strangers to celebrities, the call to weave joy resonated with thousands.

Since 2015, The Magic Yarn Project has created and deliv-ered thousands of wigs worldwide, logging more than 400,000 volunteer hours. Each wig is handmade, each one carrying the love of dozens of hands and hearts.

"There are days I wonder, *'They're just wigs, does this really matter?'*" Holly admits. "Then we get a note from a parent who says, *'My daughter smiled again today,'* or a family who shares that their child was buried in her favorite wig. And I know, it matters more than we'll ever realize."

What began as one act of kindness became a lifeline for families walking through some of their darkest days. For the children, the wigs aren't just playful costumes; they're a shield of courage, a way to face needles and treatments with a spark of joy. And for families, each handmade gift is proof that they are not alone, that an invisible circle of kindness holds them up.

From one little girl's smile to a global movement, Holly's vision continues to weave magic across the world, one strand of yarn and one spark of hope at a time.

(MKRO Kindness Grant Winner, Jul 2025)

Reflection: Holly turned a simple ball of yarn into a source of courage and joy for children battling cancer. How might your kindness change your community if practiced consistently?

Kindness Is Available To Every
Single One Of Us, No Matter
Who We Are, Where We Come From,
Or What We Have Been Through.

– Unknown

SECOND CHANCES

I n 2011, Stephen Knight's life had unraveled. At fifty-one years old, he was battling a meth addiction that had cost him everything—his career, his family, his home, and nearly his life. Alone, HIV-positive, and living out of his car, he hit rock bottom and finally decided to enter rehab.

Recovery wasn't quick or easy, but eight months in, something happened that would change his life forever.

A close friend, who had herself relapsed, showed up at his door in tears. She was desperate, ready to go back into treatment, but she wasn't empty-handed. Cradled in her arms was Jayde, a fifteen-pound Maltese-Dachshund mix with big brown eyes and a trusting little heart. With no one to care for her dog, her only option was to surrender Jayde to a shelter.

Stephen remembers the moment vividly. "I looked at Jayde, and we looked at each other," he recalls. "It was one of the most spiritual moments of my life, like we both knew we might need each other here."

Without a second thought, he said, "I'll take her."

That single, compassionate decision became the spark for Dogs Matter, the nonprofit Stephen would go on to found in 2015. At first, he thought he was simply helping out a friend. But caring for Jayde, opened his eyes: so many people were putting off addiction treatment, because they couldn't bear the thought of losing their pets. These dogs weren't just pets; they were family, comfort, and unconditional love during their darkest days.

Stephen knew this struggle all too well. Recovery asks people to give up so much: their substances, their routines, often their jobs, and sometimes even their homes. To ask them to give up their beloved companions, too, was a cruelty that made sobriety feel impossible.

So he built a program to change that. Dogs Matter provides temporary foster care for pets while their owners are in residential treatment. The dogs are cared for, loved, and safe, every expense covered, so their humans can focus on healing. When treatment ends, the program doesn't stop there. Owners are supported with a twelve-month aftercare program to help them stay strong in recovery, all while receiving regular photos and updates of their furry friends.

The results have been profound. "It gives them so much hope," Stephen says. "The bond between humans and their animals makes such a difference in recovery. People were staying sober. People had purpose."

One participant described the experience in words that could belong to so many others: "Through all the times I felt like I didn't deserve love, my dog Remy loved me anyway. I didn't want to lose him. Then somebody told me about Dogs Matter. I had no idea how much help it would bring into my life. I'd flip through the photos of him every day, and it reminded me I was doing the right thing."

Since its founding, Dogs Matter has helped more than 2,500 dogs and their owners stay together through recovery. Volunteers across Texas open their homes to foster dogs, knowing they're saving two lives at once. "Without them," Stephen says, "we couldn't do this mission."

Today, Stephen is fourteen years sober. He serves as a Substance Abuse Counselor and Program Director at Legacy Cares, guiding others through the same journey he once walked. At his side are his three dogs Piper, Lady, and Jayde, the little pup whose presence inspired a movement.

Because of one moment of connection, one man looking into the eyes of one small dog, thousands of lives have been transformed. Dogs Matter is living proof that sometimes the love of a dog is the bridge that carries a person back to themselves.

(MKRO Kindness Grant Winner, May 2025)

Reflection: Stephen's story shows how one small act of compassion grew into a life-changing mission for thousands of people and their pets. What is one simple act of kindness you could take today that might grow into something bigger than you ever imagined?

*Even if we disagree about everything,
we can still be kind to each other.*

– Matthew L. Jacobson

A SANCTUARY BUILT BY LOVE

It all began with a moment of fear and heartbreak. Jamie Wallace Griner's six-year-old son, newly diagnosed with autism, had fled a birthday party after someone said something that pierced his sensitive little heart. Jamie searched frantically until she found him, curled in the fetal position, hiding in the back of a stranger's car under the unforgiving Texas sun. That was the night everything changed.

Jamie, already familiar with the ups and downs of autism, realized she needed something more to help him navigate a world that often felt too loud, too fast, and too chaotic. That night, she began researching autism service dogs. She sent out hundreds of emails, simply signing off as "a desperate mom, determined to show up for her son, no matter what that looks like."

Only one person responded.

There was a dog, a large, white, fluffy girl named Angel, who had been trained for another child, but was considered a failure. She didn't meet the family's expectations, so they gave up on her. But Jamie saw something else. She told her son, Jackson, that Angel also had autism. That Angel understood the chaos in his heart and mind. That her job was to keep him safe and be his best friend.

When Jackson and Angel finally met, it was an instant connection. He ran to her. She ran to him. In that single moment, their lives, and countless others, were transformed.

Over the next six weeks, Angel became Jackson's anchor. She calmed him in moments of sensory overload. She learned his patterns, kept him safe, and loved him with a fierce, silent intuition. One day, during a meltdown in the car, Jackson began to hurt himself. Without waiting for a command, Angel climbed through the vehicle, over two other kids, and lay her body gently across his arms. At first, he was shocked, but then he was relieved. Her weight was all he needed. He stopped. He breathed. And from that day forward, he never had another self-harming breakdown while Angel was alive.

That bond became the heartbeat of what would eventually grow into Safe in Austin, a nonprofit animal sanctuary nestled in the heart of Texas, dedicated to rescuing animals with special needs and connecting them with children who need them even more.

Today, Safe in Austin is home to over two hundred rescued animals, many blind, deaf, missing limbs, diabetic, or recovering from severe abuse. Kids with autism, anxiety, trauma, physical disabilities, and emotional scars come here, and magic happens. Together, they heal in ways that defy explanation.

Visitors meet animals who reflect their own struggles. A child in a wheelchair may meet a goat in a wheelchair. A burn survivor may hug a puppy who was pulled from a dumpster with matching scars. Nonverbal children can speak their first words to a gentle horse. Survivors of abuse can sit quietly beside therapy dogs who have survived the same.

Safe in Austin isn't just a sanctuary. It's a living, breathing reminder that healing happens through unconditional love, and animals are often the best teachers of that truth.

Jamie often jokes that 50% of her life is cleaning up poop, and 48% is begging for donations to meet the growing need. But the 2% remaining? That's magic, the quiet moments of connection, hope, and healing that happen every single day.

What started with one misunderstood dog and one overwhelmed little boy has become a sanctuary for thousands. A place where kindness lives, love is given freely, and no one is ever asked to earn their worth.

With Safe in Austin, Jamie built a haven where hurting hearts, human and animal alike, can find healing, together.

(MKRO Kindness Grant Winner, Feb 2022)

Reflection: Jamie's journey began with seeing how Angel transformed her son's life, leading her to create a safe haven where animals and people heal together. How might you take a challenge or personal experience in your own life and turn it into a source of healing or hope for others?

*Act as if what you do makes
a difference. It does.*

– William James

THE EVERLASTING HUG

On a chilly evening in 2015, Barbara Buckley sat at her kitchen table, her hands resting on a soft piece of fleece. Across from her, her great-nieces, the Varney sisters, were quietly cutting and tying the edges. The house was filled with an aching silence. Just weeks earlier, their world had been shattered when Annie, the girls' mother and Barbara's niece, lost her battle with depression and died by suicide at just thirty-five years old.

Grief hung heavy in the room like an uninvited guest. But as they worked, something gentle began to stir. The blanket they were making wasn't just fabric knotted together; it was a memory, a feeling, a way to hold onto Annie's warmth. Annie had always given the best hugs, the kind that wrapped you up completely and made you feel safe. "What if we could give those hugs to others?" Barbara whispered. And with that thought, Annie's Kindness Blankets was born.

At first, the family's goal was simple: make thirty-five blankets, one for each year of Annie's life. They wanted to help heal their own broken hearts, and along the way, let thirty-five strangers know they weren't alone in their pain. Each blanket would be tied by hand, placed in a tote bag, and marked with a label promoting kindness, a message of hope stitched into every corner.

Then something remarkable happened. When the first blankets were delivered, the response was overwhelming. Recipients clutched them tightly, some with tears in their eyes, saying it really did feel like being wrapped in an "everlasting hug." Parents told Barbara that the blankets opened the door to conversations about feelings and mental health. Families shared that in moments of deep struggle, the blanket was a source of comfort and connection.

"By putting Annie in front of us, and not behind us, telling her story, and sending out some love," Barbara explained, "we helped others know that it's okay to not be okay. They matter."

What began as thirty-five blankets exploded into more than 24,000, created by an army of volunteers from every walk of life: kindergarteners, Girl Scouts, sports teams, college students, corporate groups, even strangers who simply wanted to help. Every blanket carried Annie's spirit forward, wrapping someone in comfort during their darkest hours.

But the magic wasn't just in the fleece. In gyms, classrooms, and church basements, people gathered to tie strips of fabric, and while their hands were busy, their hearts were opening. Parents talked to kids about mental health. Teens shared struggles they hadn't dared speak aloud. Teachers listened to students in ways they hadn't before. In these small circles, the stigma around depression and suicide began to loosen.

Partnerships have spread the love even further. With Sleep in Heavenly Peace, children who received new beds also got an Annie's Kindness Blanket to tuck them in. Foster children celebrating birthdays with Simon Says Give unwrapped not only toys, but a blanket stitched with love. Each collaboration extends Annie's hug a little farther into the world.

Though nothing can bring Annie back, Barbara and her great-nieces know she is still changing lives. "Helping others gives us peace and keeps her spirit alive in our hearts," Barbara says softly.

Annie's Kindness Blankets is more than fleece and thread. It is grief transformed into love. It is a reminder that even in our darkest moments, kindness has the power to reach in, lift us up, and whisper: you are not alone.

(MKRO Kindness Grant Winner, May 2024)

Reflection: Barbara and her great-nieces turned unimaginable grief into a movement of comfort and compassion, reminding people they are not alone. How might you honor the memory of someone you've lost, or transform your own pain, into an act of kindness that ripples out to others?

I've learned that when you don't know what to do next, helping someone else often helps you, too. Somehow, it eases your own pain, at least for a while. It gives you a sense of purpose when you feel helpless.

– Maria Shriver

FROM WASTE
TO HOPE

George Ahearn will never forget the scene that first broke his heart. A field in eastern Washington, stretching as far as the eye could see, littered with piles of perfectly good potatoes and onions, vegetables that had been grown with care, harvested with hope, and then abandoned. Farmers were plowing them back into the soil, not because they were spoiled, but because there was no market for them. At the same time, George knew families only a few hours away who were standing in line at food banks, desperate to put dinner on the table.

The sight hit him like a gut punch. How could mountains of food sit discarded while children went to bed hungry? George didn't have a plan, but he had a conviction: this isn't right, and I have to do something about it.

At first, his idea seemed simple. He would collect the unsold crops and deliver them directly to food banks. Easy, right? But reality quickly humbled him. Farmers weren't talking about a few bags of produce; they were talking about truckloads. And food banks? They couldn't accept unwashed or unpackaged crops. And George's personal vehicle was no match for tons of onions and potatoes. What began as an instinctive gesture of kindness suddenly looked like an impossible logistical nightmare.

But George didn't give up. Instead, he reached out for help. He posted on Facebook, explaining the heartbreaking problem: WASTED FOOD! Farmers were being forced to destroy good food while families went hungry. That single post sparked a chain reaction. Two strangers, Nancy Balin and Zsofia Pasztor, jumped in to help. Nancy organized convoys of trucks to haul the food. Zsofia rallied an army of volunteers, people who stood shoulder to shoulder packaging onions and potatoes, and preparing thousands of pounds of produce for distribution.

Their very first effort moved nearly nine and a half tons of food. George thought they had solved the problem; surely this would be enough to overwhelm his local food banks. But within two days, every last potato and onion was gone. The need was staggering, far greater than he imagined. And in that moment, he realized this wasn't a one-time mission. It was the beginning of something much bigger.

From the start, George was determined to honor farmers as well as feed families. "I wasn't about to ask my farming community, the people I grew up around, to just give it all away," he explained. "I wanted to cover their costs whenever possible. This had to be fair for everyone." That simple principle, dignity and sustainability on both sides, became the foundation of what would grow into East West Food Rescue. What started as three people trying to solve a local problem quickly snowballed into a regional movement. Convoys crisscrossed Washington and neighboring states. Volunteers packed food by the ton. Farmers saw their hard work put to good use, and families who had been staring at empty cupboards suddenly had fresh produce in their kitchens.

In just five years, East West Food Rescue has moved nearly seventy-two million pounds of food, a number so vast it's hard to picture. But behind every pound is a human story: a farmer who didn't have to watch his harvest rot, a mother who could cook dinner without wondering what to feed her children, a community reminded of the power of working together.

George never set out to start a nonprofit. He just saw a problem and refused to look away. And in doing so, he proved something quite extraordinary: one small act of kindness can ripple outward until it becomes a movement, nourishing not just bodies, but dignity, hope, and community.

(MKRO Kindness Grant Winner, Aug 2022)

> **Reflection:** George's compassion shows how one person's determination can restore dignity to those too often forgotten. What kind of difference do you want your kindness to make in the long run?

In the constant pursuit of more and better, we can easily lose sight of the everyday riches that lie right in front of us and within us.

– Guri Mehta

SERVING SECOND CHANCES

❤

The smell of fresh dough and bubbling cheese greets you the moment you walk into Down North Pizza in Philadelphia. Laughter drifts from the kitchen, where cooks joke with one another as they slide pies from the oven. On the surface, it looks like any other bustling neighborhood pizzeria. But if you pause for a moment, you realize there's something different happening here, something quietly revolutionary.

Muhammad Abdul-Hadi, the restaurant's founder, remembers the moment it all began. He had just purchased a rundown building in a neighborhood that had seen better days. As he walked the block, he noticed the boarded-up storefronts, the empty lots, the families trying to make do in a food desert where fresh, affordable meals were nearly impossible to find. "My intent," Muhammad said, "was always to bring something there that would uplift and serve the community, not just take from it."

But as he began shaping his vision for the restaurant, life threw him a curveball. He faced his own set of legal troubles, and it opened his eyes to just how stacked the system was against people coming home from prison. No job without an address, no address without a job. Employers tossing applications in the trash the moment they saw the checked box for a criminal record. It was a cycle designed to trap people in failure.

"I knew this was where I could make change," Muhammad said. "Reducing recidivism became the mission for Down North Pizza. I wanted to build something that could rewrite that story."

And he did. Today, Down North Pizza exclusively hires formerly incarcerated people, giving them not just a paycheck, but a real pathway. Employees learn culinary skills, but they also gain life skills, how to manage money, navigate transportation, or access housing. Apartments above the restaurant provide stability, while pro bono legal services give staff a chance to start fresh. It's like a full-service life reboot, plus pizza.

For people like Mike Carter, now thirty-seven, that fresh start was life-changing. He had been in and out of jail since he was sixteen, worn down by the stigma that followed him everywhere. "We are not our worst mistakes," Mike said quietly, recalling how many doors had slammed shut in his face before Muhammad gave him a chance. Today, he's the executive chef of Down North Pizza, running a kitchen where his team isn't just making food, they're making a future.

The transformation is visible in the small things: the way staff members greet each other like family, the pride in serving a customer, the sound of laughter echoing off the restaurant's walls. These moments aren't just byproducts of a successful business; they're proof that dignity, belonging, and hope can be restored when someone chooses to believe in you.

"What drives me," Muhammad said, "is creating opportunities for the people around me and giving them the tools and resources to succeed. Seeing staff laugh, knowing they come from the same struggle but have a life to look forward to, that's what matters."

The ripple is spreading. Down North Pizza has already inspired others to reexamine hiring practices and think about the role of business in breaking cycles of injustice. Muhammad's nonprofit, the Down North Foundation, now funds youth programs and other initiatives to stop recidivism before it begins.

He has big dreams of expanding to other underserved communities across the U.S. "What I'm doing alongside my team is not hard," he said. "It's just."

Down North Pizza proves that business can do more than make money; it can heal, restore, and rewrite lives. In every slice served, there's a second chance, and in every laugh from the kitchen, the sound of freedom finding its way home.

(MKRO Kindness Award Winner, Dec 2024)

Reflection: Muhammad saw brokenness in his community and chose to respond with opportunity, dignity, and hope. How might you create space in your own life, or in your community, for forgiveness, second chances, and new beginnings?

My religion is very simple.
My religion is kindness.

– The Dalai Lama

CHANGING YOUNG LIVES

On a quiet winter morning in Canton, Ohio, the halls of a local elementary school felt heavier than usual. Teachers whispered, students sensed the tension, and an unshakable grief hung in the air. Within a single school year, the district had lost six students to suicide. For many, it was unimaginable. For Mindy Ousley, a 4th-grade teacher, it was painfully personal. These weren't just numbers or headlines; these were children. Children who had once laughed in the cafeteria, drawn crayon rainbows in class, and played tag at recess. Now they were gone.

Mindy stood in her classroom, looking at her students, and felt a knot in her chest. What if one of *these* children someday believed they didn't matter? What if silence and isolation continued to swallow them before they could reach out for help? The thought was unbearable. She knew she couldn't erase the pain, but she could plant something different in its place: hope.

So, she started small. She gathered a group of 3rd and 4th-graders one afternoon and asked them a simple question: What if kindness was our mission? The students leaned in, eyes wide and curious. From that question, The Kindness Club was born.

At first, the projects were simple. Students made colorful posters with hand-drawn hearts and cheerful words like "You Matter" and "You Belong Here." They taped them to the hallways, turning dull walls into daily reminders that love was stronger than despair. But once the kids caught the kindness bug, it spread fast.

One Friday night, a bunch of club members stood at the entrance of a football game, nervously clutching stacks of handwritten notes. Each note carried a few heartfelt words:

"You are loved."

"We're glad you're here."

"Don't give up."

As fans streamed through the gates, the children held out their notes with shy smiles. Parents stopped mid-step, some blinking back tears. One mother clutched a note to her chest and whispered, "You don't know how much I needed this tonight." In that moment, the kids realized their small gestures could touch hearts they'd never imagined.

The ripple only grew. The club partnered with a homeless shelter, creating bright placemats covered in doodles and encouraging words. When the meals were served, shelter residents paused, staring at the colorful creations made just for them. Some laughed, some cried, and one man folded his placemat carefully and tucked it into his pocket to keep. Another month, the students decorated meal delivery bags for homebound patients.

What had begun as a small classroom idea was reaching far beyond the school walls. In just one year, Mindy's Kindness Club had touched more than 3,000 lives. Andi it wasn't just the world outside changing, the kids themselves were changing, too. Shy students found their voices. Kids who felt invisible suddenly realized they could lead change. Kindness, Mindy realized, wasn't just healing the community; it was healing the children who carried it forward.

The biggest challenge, however, was keeping the program afloat. Supplies cost money, markers, poster boards, craft materials, and Mindy quietly covered much of it herself. When donations trickled in, she stretched every dollar, determined never to let finances stop the flow of kindness. That's why the MKRO Kindness Grant was so meaningful. It wasn't just about money; it was recognition that her mission mattered. That the lives of her students, and the lives they touched, were worth investing in.

For Mindy, The Kindness Club was never about projects on paper. It was about planting seeds in young hearts that would keep growing long after they left her classroom. "Kindness is power," she told her students. "It's how we change the world, one person at a time."

And in a community shaken by loss, Mindy's determination reminded everyone that while tragedy may leave deep scars, kindness has the strength to stitch us back together.

(MKRO Kindness Grant Winner, Aug 2019)

> **Reflection:** Mindy turned unimaginable loss into a living lesson of hope, showing her students that kindness is a powerful antidote to despair. Why do you think kindness is such a powerful response to despair?

Your beliefs don't make you a better person; your behavior does.

– Sukhraj S. Dhillon

A CHAPTER OF KINDNESS

Cedric sat stiffly in his chair, staring at the book in front of him as though the words had betrayed him. The characters' names, the plot he had read just last week, it was all gone, slipping through his mind like sand through an open palm. At seventy-two years old, with an early-stage dementia diagnosis, he had come to the Ed Brown Senior Center on his doctor's advice. A book club, they said, would be good for him. But now, surrounded by strangers, his heart sank. He hated the feeling of being the man who couldn't keep up.

He glanced at the clock, already counting the minutes until he could leave.

And then the door swung open.

A teenager walked in, bright and confident, her youth striking against a room otherwise filled with gray hair, walkers, and wheelchairs. Cedric lowered his eyes, embarrassed at the thought of having to introduce himself. But instead of hesitating, the girl walked right up to him, extended both hands, and said with a bright, steady smile, "I'm Jessica. I'm here to talk about books. I'm glad to meet you."

Something shifted.

Cedric remembered how, in recent months, people often spoke around him rather than to him, like he was invisible, or worse, like a child who needed constant supervision. But here was Jessica, looking him in the eyes, speaking to him with warmth and respect. For the first time in a long time, he felt seen.

That moment, so small on the surface, was the beginning of something extraordinary. Jessica didn't stop with one book club visit. What started as a single gesture grew into a mission. She now runs multiple book clubs at senior centers throughout San Diego, spaces where laughter mixes with literature, and where men and women who often feel forgotten are reminded that they still matter.

She tutors after school to earn money, not to spend on teenage luxuries, but to pay for Uber rides so she can get to the centers. She could have chosen clothes, gadgets, or outings with friends, but instead, she chose connection. She chose to sit with people like Cedric, to listen, to encourage, to remind them they are not alone.

"She's made hundreds of seniors remember that we matter," Cedric wrote when he nominated her for the MKRO Kindness Award. "She smiles when others criticize her book choices. She shakes all of our hands after the meetings. She does it all out of kindness."

And then Cedric said something even more moving and profound:

"She changed my life. I know I might not remember writing this, but that doesn't mean this writing is meaningless. She cares about me and others. She values what I have to say. I know I am loved."

Jessica Ong was only seventeen years old, but her kindness carried the weight of something timeless. She gave dignity back to people who felt it slipping away. She reminded them that their voices still mattered, that they still belonged.

Her story is proof that kindness doesn't require years of wisdom or vast resources; it only requires a willing heart. One teenager walked into a room, extended her hands, and in doing so, opened a door for hundreds of others to step back into themselves.

Jessica's story will stay with us, like the best books do, long after the final page is turned.

(MKRO Kindness Award Winner, Nov 2022)

> **Reflection:** Jessica's story shows how small acts of genuine connection can bring dignity and joy to those often overlooked. How does this story change your understanding of what it means to be a kindness hero? What small step could you take to start your own ripple?

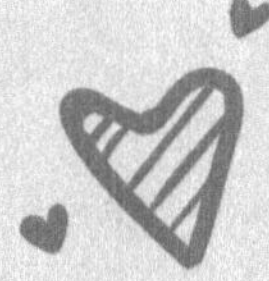

Kindness is not just a choice; it's a lifestyle. Every act, big or small, creates a ripple effect of positivity. Join us in making the world a brighter place.

– Zachery Dereniowski

FILLING THE GAP

Sometimes change doesn't come with a big fanfare or a drumroll. Sometimes it sneaks in quietly, like a worried glance, a whispered conversation, or noticing a neighbor in need. For Ashley and Dustin Beeler, it began with a simple, and painful, truth: hunger was too close to home to ignore.

They often passed the same street corner where a man slept on a bench, wrapped in a thin blanket against the cold. They'd see others huddled in doorways, carrying their lives in worn-out bags, their faces etched with exhaustion. They noticed lines of people at soup kitchens.

Ashley couldn't shake the images. At home one evening, she and Dustin talked about it at the kitchen table seeing the daily struggles of people in their community, people who felt invisible in their struggles.

"These are our neighbors," Dustin said. "We don't have a lot of time, and our budgets are nearly maxed out. But we can't ignore the need."

That conversation became the seed of something extraordinary.

Drawing inspiration from the Little Free Library movement, Ashley and Dustin decided to try a pantry version: the Little Free Pantry. They scraped together enough money to build the first small wooden box, painting it a cheerful color and installing it on the edge of their neighborhood. Inside, they placed a few cans of soup, some granola bars, soap, and toothpaste. They attached a handwritten sign that read simply:

"Take what you need. Leave what you can."

The next day, someone had taken a can of soup and left behind a box of pasta. By the end of the week, the pantry had become a quiet little hub of care. Parents grabbed cereal for their kids. An elderly neighbor left jars of homemade jam. A teenager slipped in packs of diapers. It wasn't just food being shared; it was dignity, trust, and connection.

Word spread quickly. Two local churches soon built pantries of their own, multiplying the impact. Then, with the help of a MKRO Kindness Grant, Ashley and Dustin were able to expand even further. One pantry was placed at the Recovery Alliance, where families struggling with addiction often found themselves without basic necessities. Another landed in a rural food desert, where grocery stores were miles away, but need was right at their doorstep.

In both places, the results were immediate. Struggling single mothers were able to make dinner for their kids. A man who had been skipping meals to stretch his limited income was finally able to eat regularly.

What started as a single wooden box became a ripple of kindness stretching across their community. And even more powerful than the food was the spirit it sparked. Neighbors who might not have spoken before now greeted each other while restocking shelves. Strangers became friends through the quiet, shared act of caring.

Ashley and Dustin often remind people, "We're not an organization. We're not a nonprofit. We're neighbors." And that is exactly what makes their work so moving. With little more than heart, determination, and the courage to act, they showed their town that ordinary people can create extraordinary change.

The Little Free Pantry is more than stocked shelves; it's hope in a box, reminding us all that kindness, even in the smallest gestures, has the power to nourish not just bodies, but hearts.

(MKRO Kindness Grant Winner, Aug 2019)

Reflection: Ashley and Dustin remind us that even with limited resources, kindness has the power to ripple far beyond what we might imagine. What's one small act of generosity you could offer your community that might create ripples of change?

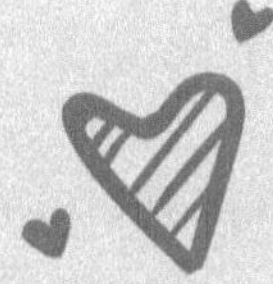

Being kind may not make us successful or rich or heroic, but being kind does make us a little happier and someone else's day a little better, and really, that's saying something. Kindness is our gift to one another, to the world, and to our own best selves.

– Katrina Kenison

SERVING HOPE

On a bitterly cold Friday night in upstate New York, a line starts forming under the glow of a single streetlight in Albany. The people waiting aren't here for a handout; they're here for something far more vital: warmth, dignity, and the reminder that they matter. At the front of the line, Renee and Mike Fahey greet each person by name, their car trunks and folding tables transformed into a lifeline of hot meals, clothing, and kindness.

It wasn't always this way. Back in 2016, Street Soldiers began with nothing more than a 4x4 card table, a box of sandwiches, and a pot of soup. "I don't think either one of us pictured where it would lead," Mike said. But on that very first night, as they handed out food to people who hadn't eaten all day, something shifted. Renee remembers watching one man cradle his sandwich as if it were pure treasure. "It was like we had given him a feast," she said. "That's when I knew we had to keep coming back."

And so they did. Every Friday night, no matter the weather, (and upstate New York isn't exactly known for gentle winters) Renee and Mike show up, after loading their cars from a garage packed to the ceiling with donated coats, coolers full of drinks, and cars stuffed with tables, socks, and hygiene kits. Their home has become a staging ground for compassion, their driveway a revolving door for volunteers who load up and head out into the streets.

Pretty quickly, they realized the need was way bigger than they could have imagined. More and more faces began showing up each week, people who had lost jobs, parents with children in tow, elderly neighbors living in their cars. Some came for a hot meal, but many came for something even simpler - human connection. "What people want most isn't just food," Renee said. "It's someone looking them in the eye and saying, 'I see you. You matter.'"

There are moments that stick. Like the time Renee slipped a pair of clean socks into a man's hands. He held them to his chest and was so grateful. One small, ordinary thing, socks, became a lifeline. Stories like this happen again and again: a teenager smiling over a warm plate of pasta, a woman tearing up at the gift of a winter coat, a man hearing his name spoken with care for the first time in months.

Street Soldiers has grown into much more than just a food distribution effort. It's a place where people feel safe, where laughter and music mingle with the clatter of serving spoons, and where strangers quickly become family. The Fahey's believe that small, consistent kindness builds trust, and trust is what creates hope.

Their motto is simple: "We can't change the world, but we can help those locals who are a part of the world. We do what we can, when we can."

And in doing so, they've sparked something bigger. Volunteers return week after week, inspired by Renee and Mike's unwavering commitment. What started as one card table has become a movement, proving that kindness doesn't need a budget, only a willing heart.

Through Street Soldiers, Renee and Mike have shown that kindness is never wasted. One warm meal, one pair of socks, one kind word at a time, they are rewriting the story of what it means to show up for one another.

(MKRO Kindness Award Winner, Nov 2019)

Reflection: Renee and Mike show us that kindness doesn't require perfection or wealth, just a willingness to show up for those who need it most. How does practicing kindness change the way you see yourself?

Kindness is an active choice to see someone's dignity and respond to them in a way that speaks to the wholeness of who they are.

– Alyson Stoner

FROM ER TO EMPOWERMENT

❤

One night in the ER, a teenage girl sat across from nurse practitioner Jessica Muñoz, her arms wrapped tightly around herself like she was trying to disappear. She wouldn't make eye contact. Her clothes were torn, her voice barely a whisper. On paper, she looked like just another patient. But Jessica's instincts told her otherwise. This wasn't neglect this was exploitation. As she leaned in gently, asking the questions no one else had thought to ask, the truth came out. The girl was a victim of sex trafficking.

Jessica never forgot that night, nor the dozens of others that followed. Young girls and boys slipping through the cracks, carrying wounds no medical chart could capture. What haunted her most wasn't just the violence these children endured, but how often the systems meant to protect them failed to see the signs. Children were sent back into danger, treated as problems to fix instead of lives to heal.

Instead of turning away, Jessica made a choice: she would fight for them and shine a light so bright it would make it hard for anyone to look away.

That choice became Hoʻōla Nā Pua: "New Life for Our Children." Jessica founded the nonprofit with the purpose of supporting healing and restoration to children rescued from trafficking. Jessica envisioned a place where survivors weren't just stabilized but empowered, where they could rebuild their sense of safety, self-worth, and purpose.

Her vision came to life in Pearl Haven, a 32-bed residential treatment campus for girls ages 11–18, the first of its kind in Hawaiʻi and one of only a handful in the nation. More than a shelter, Pearl Haven is a sanctuary and a model of care that had not existed before. Behind its doors, children who once knew only fear are learning to laugh again. They attend classes, share meals, create art, and slowly, tenderly, rediscover what it means to feel safe.

Jessica has walked beside countless survivors in their darkest moments. She knows the weight of their stories, the nightmares that still wake them, and the way trust must be rebuilt one fragile step at a time.

"It's a marathon, not a sprint," she said. "But the resilient hope of these kids is what keeps me going. They are stronger than anyone realizes."

Jessica's impact doesn't stop at Pearl Haven. She has become a national and international voice for the invisible, urging policymakers, law enforcement, and communities to see what she saw that night in the ER: children who need someone to notice them before it's too late. Her leadership has sparked real change, strengthened protections, and expanded awareness across Hawaiʻi and beyond.

The ripple effect is profound: families reunited, survivors finding their voices, communities better equipped to respond and prevent exploitation. Each child who enters Pearl Haven carries a story of trauma, but they leave with a renewed sense of possibility, hope, and a bright future.

Jessica's courage reminds us that kindness is not passive. It's fierce, determined, and stubbornly refuses to accept a world where children are bought and sold. Standing with the most vulnerable, Jessica is more than a leader, she is a lifeline. A steady hand pulling kids from the shadows into the light. Her story reminds us all: when you choose to see, you can change everything.

(MKRO Kindness Award Winner, Nov 2019)

> **Reflection:** Jessica's work highlights the healing power of compassion for people who have endured unimaginable pain. What's one way you can show support to someone in your community who may feel unseen or unheard?

You cannot go through a single day without having an impact on the world around you. What you do makes a difference, and you have to decide what kind of difference you want to make.

– Jane Goodall

CATIO MAGIC

The cat room at the Marshmallow Foundation is usually a symphony of meows, some soft and curious, others desperate for attention. On any given day, fifty to eighty cats live in this small space, all waiting for someone to choose them and bring them home. But despite the chorus of voices, there is only one small window in the room, a single square of light that the cats compete for. They crowd against it, noses pressed to the glass, as if hoping the world outside might somehow be theirs, too.

For Connie Hammes, that window was heartbreaking. A lifelong volunteer, animal lover, and a part-time worker at the Marshmallow Foundation, Connie had a special tenderness for the cats. She noticed how some would pace restlessly, how others grew lethargic from the monotony of confinement. A few developed behavior issues, not because they were "bad cats," but because they were stressed and longing for something more.

One afternoon, she paused to watch a small gray tabby crouched by the window, batting at the shadow of a bird fluttering past. The cat's tail flicked with intensity; her entire body was alive with the instinct to chase. But then the bird was gone, and the tabby returned to her corner, her eyes dull again. That moment stayed with Connie. These animals deserved more than four walls and a single sliver of sunlight.

That's when she had an idea: a Catio.

A Catio, short for "cat patio," is a screened-in outdoor enclosure that allows cats to safely experience the outdoors, the breeze in their fur, the warmth of the sun, the sounds of leaves and birds, without the dangers of running off or encountering other animals. It was such a simple concept, but for shelter cats, it could mean everything.

When Connie found out she was awarded the MKRO Kindness Grant, she wasted no time making her dream a reality. She enlisted local builder, Kory Bartsch, who generously donated his skills. Together, they began to build. With every post secured and every screen stretched tight, Connie pictured the cats' first steps into the fresh air, the joy it would bring them.

The day the Catio opened, Connie stood by the doorway, heart racing, as the first group of cats cautiously explored the new space. One ginger tomcat stretched out in a patch of sunlight, closing his eyes in pure contentment. Two kittens darted back and forth, chasing each other through grass-like mats. Others perched on shelves; ears perked at the sound of birdsong. For the first time, these cats were not just surviving, they were thriving.

Connie's small act of kindness rippled far beyond that little outdoor space. Healthier, happier cats meant fewer behavior problems, making them more adoptable. Families who came to the shelter now met animals who were calmer, friendlier, and ready to love. And for the cats still waiting, the Catio offered a sanctuary, a reminder that even in transition, their lives had value.

All of this happened because one volunteer noticed a need and cared enough to do something about it. Connie saw more than cats in cages; she saw lives waiting for sunlight, fresh air, and joy. And with her dedication, she gave them just that.

(MKRO Kindness Grant Winner, Feb 2019)

> **Reflection:** Connie's love for animals shows how one person's creativity and compassion can dramatically improve the lives of shelter pets. Is there a kindness project or volunteer opportunity you've always wanted to try but haven't begun? What's holding you back? Take one small step this week toward making it real.

Kindness is the best balm for psychic wounds; it helps both the giver and the recipient.

– Monica Hess

WHERE KINDNESS BEGINS

♥

There's a special kind of joy that comes from being kind: it warms your chest, makes your heart do a little happy dance, and leaves you wanting to do it all over again. For seventeen-year-old Shreyaa Venkat, those "kindness hits" first came from volunteering at schools, libraries, senior homes, and community events. Each time she helped someone, she felt her heart expand, as if kindness itself was contagious. The more she gave, the more she wanted to give. What began as small acts of service quickly became a calling: to spread kindness as far and wide as she could, and to inspire others to do the same.

So naturally, she teamed up with her sister, Esha Venkat, and co-founded NEST4US, a nonprofit built on the belief that kindness should be woven into everyday life. What started as two sisters looking for ways to give back has blossomed into a movement, mobilizing thousands of volunteers, building partnerships with different sectors, and empowering the next generation to make service a part of who they are.

Along the way, they discovered a little secret: kindness doesn't just change the lives of those receiving it; it transforms the lives of those giving, too. Every care package assembled, every meal served, every handwritten note tucked inside a bag became another ripple of hope. Volunteers caught the same "kindness bug" that Shreyaa had first discovered, and suddenly, kindness wasn't just something you do, it was something you lived by.

Through NEST4US, meals are shared, care packages are assembled, and backpacks filled with toiletries and nonperishable food find their way into the hands of families who otherwise might go without. During the height of the COVID-19 pandemic, when isolation and fear hung heavy in the air, Shreyaa and her team delivered not just supplies, but hope. Over 10,000 handwritten notes of encouragement were tucked inside packages, a quiet but powerful reminder to strangers that they were seen and loved.

One mother, opening a box of food with her two young children, found a note that read, "Stay strong, brighter days are ahead." The mother later told volunteers it was the first time in months she felt hopeful enough to believe it.

Shreyaa's vision has always gone beyond charity; it's about connection. She and Esha launched programs like NEST Nurtures, which provides nutritious foods to low-income families, and NEST Tutors, offering free academic support for children struggling in school. They've since branched out to more programs, such as their NEST Kares kindness program, NEST Buddies birthday-in-a-box program, and a NEST Inspires leadership program, all aimed at creating more opportunities for communities to put kindness into practice and make a powerful difference far and wide.

For Shreyaa, each innovation circles back to that same lesson she learned when she first started volunteering: kindness is most powerful when it's personal.

"Giving back helps us grow and gain a different perspective on things often taken for granted," Shreyaa and Esha say. "We strongly believe that even if you have nothing else to give, your kindness means the world."

Here's the kicker: she started NEST4US at thirteen. Thirteen! While most of us were stressing over whether to add extra sprinkles on our cupcakes, Shreyaa was organizing volunteers, delivering meals, and teaching the world that age is no excuse not to make a difference.

But perhaps the true beauty of her work lies not in the impressive numbers, the tens of thousands of meals served, the thousands of volunteers mobilized, but in the quiet, human moments: a child smiling at a stranger's note, a man holding a scrap of paper like treasure, a family feeling hope again.

Because for Shreyaa, kindness isn't about changing the whole world at once. It's about making sure no one forgets that they matter.

(MKRO Kindness Award Winner, May 2020)

Reflection: Shreyaa's story shows how one person's passion can mobilize an entire community to create waves of kindness and hope for those most in need. How have you seen kindness ripple out in your own community?

*The way you shout it into the woods
is the way it comes back to you.*

**– Romy Jaworski
(Matt's Grandmother)**

SHOPPING ANGELS

It was March 2020, and the world outside folded in on itself: empty streets, shuttered stores, and a quiet exhaustion hanging in the air. As Jayde Powell sat at the Reno-Tahoe Airport waiting for her flight back home, she found herself scrolling through news updates and social media posts filled with panic. While others scrambled to stockpile toilet paper or barricade themselves inside, Jayde felt her heart tighten at the thought of the most vulnerable: seniors, immunocompromised neighbors, and those without easy access to groceries or medicine. They were the ones truly isolated by fear and circumstance.

Her mind raced. How could she help? Just then, her phone rang. She was grateful for the chance to talk with her mom before getting on the plane. As they chatted, her mom mentioned she was about to head to the grocery store, and before hanging up, casually added that she'd check in with their elderly neighbors to see if they needed anything.

That gave her the idea: what if strangers became angels, looking out for one another when the world stopped turning normally? Jayde grabbed her phone made a social media account and posted a simple message: ""Las Vegas and Reno, Shopping Angels: A program where young adults volunteer their time to pick up your groceries and other shopping necessities, so you can stay safe at home!"

Within hours, her inbox exploded. Requests for help, offers to volunteer, people basically saying, "Where do I sign up?" By the time she had landed in Las Vegas, a local news channel had heard this message and requested an interview. This would be the gateway through which the rest of the country would hear about Shopping Angels.

That night, under the glare of her laptop screen, Jayde created a system, a simple spreadsheet, a Google form, where volunteers could sign up and be matched with neighbors in need. She reached out to friends in her medical fraternity, classmates, even complete strangers, weaving a web of kindness across the city that soon spread beyond it. In just days, hundreds were pitching in to buy groceries, pick up prescriptions, and deliver essentials, all while practicing social distancing and safety protocols.

Jayde remembers Renee, a ninety-two-year-old woman who lived alone. For Renee, Jayde's deliveries were more than food; they were a lifeline in an isolating world. "Many told me they hadn't left their homes in weeks. Some cried when they realized there was someone to help them," Jayde shared, her voice thick with emotion.

But it wasn't just groceries. Jayde saw the fear, the loneliness, and the desperate need for human connection. Volunteers went above and beyond, making phone calls just to say, "I'm here." One volunteer drove an hour and a half to deliver essentials; another scoured multiple stores to fill a single list; kindness became a lifeline, a thread holding the community together when so much threatened to tear it apart.

As Shopping Angels grew, the movement transcended Las Vegas. Branches sprouted nationwide and overseas. "It was astonishing," Jayde recalls. "The need was so much greater than I ever imagined, and the willingness to help was even bigger."

Even after the initial waves of lockdown lifted, Jayde continued to volunteer and mobilize. She spoke to groups about building lasting networks of mutual aid, neighbors who don't wait for crises but look out for each other every day. In moments when fear threatened to overwhelm, Jayde's Shopping Angels became a beacon of resilience, empathy, and the transformative power of kindness.

Jayde's story is a beautifully human reminder: When fear closes doors, kindness opens them. One young woman sitting alone in an airport terminal and a living room, chose to listen, to see, and to act. And in doing so, she lit a path for thousands who found themselves lifted, nourished, and no longer alone. It's a legacy born not of grand gestures, but of simple acts: running errands, offering a phone call, and showing up when it matters most.

(MKRO Kindness Award Winner, May 2020)

> **Reflection:** Jayde's creativity shows how kindness and innovation can spark hope during even the hardest times. How could you use your own creativity to meet a need in your community?

There's no such thing as a small act of kindness. Every act creates a ripple with no logical end.

– Scott Adams

COLORING OUTSIDE THE LINES

On her tenth birthday, when most kids dream of ripping open presents, Chelsea Phaire had something different in mind. Standing in front of her friends and family, she smiled shyly and made a simple request: "no gifts for me, bring art supplies instead." She asked for markers, crayons, sketch pads, paints, and anything that kids could use to create. Her parents exchanged surprised glances, but Chelsea's mind was already made up. She wasn't thinking about herself. She was thinking about kids she had never even met, kids in homeless shelters and foster care who, she knew, might be carrying heavy burdens with no safe way to let them out.

That day, Chelsea packed up her very first art kits and handed them to children who, at first, weren't sure what to make of them. One little girl clutched a coloring book to her chest as if it were treasure. Another boy immediately tore open the markers and went to town, sketching furiously, his face lighting up as color filled the page. It was like they've been waiting for this, waiting to be told it's okay to express what they feel. Chelsea watched quietly, a spark of determination forming inside her.

She knew what they were feeling. Chelsea had lost a loved one to gun violence when she was younger, and the grief was almost too much to carry. For her, art became a lifeline. When words failed, her drawings gave shape to the sadness and hope tangled inside her heart. She wanted these kids—kids who had been displaced, hurt, or left behind—to know they weren't alone. That's how Chelsea's Charity was born.

What began with a birthday wish quickly grew into a movement. With the help of her parents, Chelsea began sending art kits across the country to shelters, hospitals, schools, and community centers. Each kit carried more than supplies. Inside was a handwritten note: "You matter. You are loved. You are not forgotten." Those words often became the first spark of hope for kids who felt invisible.

One mom noted that her foster child hadn't spoken much since entering foster care, but after she received a kit, she spent hours and hours coloring in the book and started opening up a little. That was the power of Chelsea's kindness; art wasn't just art; it was a bridge.

As the requests poured in, Chelsea's dining room became chaos central, stacks of crayons and sketchbooks spilling across the floor. She enlisted friends to help assemble packages, each one tied together with the same thread: the belief that every child deserves a way to heal.

Soon, Chelsea expanded her vision. She began hosting art workshops at shelters and community centers. Picture a room full of children sitting cross-legged on the floor, paintbrushes in hand, their laughter rising as they traded colors and admired each other's masterpieces. These weren't just art lessons. They were moments of connection, moments that told kids who often felt invisible that they matter and they belong.

By middle school, Chelsea's Charity had delivered more than 20,000 art kits across the nation. Media outlets called her inspiring, community leaders called her extraordinary, but to Chelsea, she was just doing what felt right: helping kids feel less alone.

Those who meet her describe her as radiant and wise beyond her years, a child with an old soul and an unstoppable drive to make the world gentler. Chelsea is a Kindness Hero because she turned her own grief into generosity, transforming personal pain into a lifeline for others. Her work ripples outward still, proving that sometimes hope can be rebuilt with crayons, paint, and the kindness of a little girl who believed art could heal the world.

(MKRO Kindness Grant Winner, Aug 2020)

> **Reflection:** Chelsea proves that age is no barrier to making an extraordinary impact. What passion or hobby of yours could be turned into a gift for others?

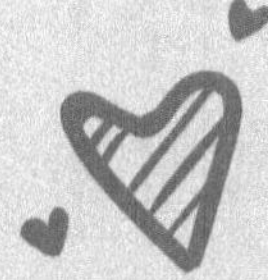

The greatness of a community is most accurately measured by the compassionate actions of its members.

– Coretta Scott King

FROM WINE NIGHT TO WETLANDS

It started with the sound of an empty wine bottle hitting the trash.

On an ordinary night in 2020, Tulane seniors Max Steitz and Franziska Trautmann sat chilling with a bottle of wine. When it was empty, Franziska held the bottle in her hands a moment longer, reluctant to toss it. She knew it was bound for a landfill, like every other glass bottle in New Orleans. The thought stung. Louisiana had no glass recycling program at the time, which meant nearly three hundred million pounds of glass every year were buried in landfills, wasted.

Frustrated, Franziska turned to Max and said what they were both already feeling: "There has to be a better way."

That bottle became the first spark of Glass Half Full, a grassroots movement that would change how an entire community thought about waste, recycling, and even the future of Louisiana's fragile coastlines.

At first, the idea seemed impossible. Two college kids weren't supposed to solve a problem that the whole state hadn't tackled. But Max and Franziska couldn't shake the image of mountains of glass piling up, while Louisiana's coast was literally disappearing, a football field of land lost to erosion every one hundred minutes. What if those two problems could solve each other? What if the glass could be turned into something useful, like sand, to help rebuild the wetlands that protect their state?

Armed with nothing but determination and a hand-crank bottle crusher, they set up shop in the backyard of a fraternity house. Friends dropped off empty beer and wine bottles. Max and Franziska went to work crushing them one by one, their hands blistered and their clothes powdered with green and brown dust. It was sweaty, dirty, exhausting work, but every bag of sand felt like proof that something bigger was possible.

Word spread. Neighbors showed up at their door with boxes of glass. Strangers slipped donations into their GoFundMe account. Volunteers lined up to help sort, crush, and haul. Soon, the little backyard couldn't contain them anymore. They moved to a small facility uptown, then a full-on warehouse on Louisa Street, humming with machines that could handle thousands of bottles a day.

And the magic? The sand didn't just sit there. In one coastal restoration project, volunteers stood shoulder to shoulder, filling heavy burlap sacks with recycled glass sand. They hauled them into the water, creating new barriers where waves had been washing land away. A few months later, grasses rooted, marsh plants popped up, and birds returned. What had been open water was turning back into living wetlands.

Today, Glass Half Full has kept more than 8 million pounds of glass out of landfills and restored thousands of square meters of coastline. Their recycled sand even gets used for disaster relief, flooring, and new glass products, closing the loop that once seemed impossible.

Still, the heart of the story is simple: two young people looked at a broken system and chose hope over despair.

"Dread, doom, and gloom tend to get us nowhere," Franziska says. "But hope, combined with action, can be one of the most powerful tools to enact change."

Max and Franziska remind us that solutions don't have to start with massive budgets or government plans. Sometimes, all it takes is a bottle of wine, a backyard full of broken glass, and the courage to see possibility where others see waste.

That's why they are Kindness Heroes: because their work isn't just about recycling glass, it's about restoring coastlines, protecting communities, and proving that small sparks of determination can ignite movements of lasting change.

(MKRO Kindness Grant Winner, Mar 2025)

> **Reflection:** Max and Franziska's story shows how determination and hope can transform one big idea into lasting change for a community and the environment. What's one local issue you care about that could use creative action, and how might you take the very first step toward making a difference?

Too often we underestimate the power of a touch, a smile, a kind word, a listening ear, an honest compliment, or the smallest act of caring, all of which have the potential to turn a life around.

– Leo Buscaglia

BEAUTY WITH PURPOSE

On a Saturday morning in downtown Los Angeles, Shirley Raines stood on the edge of a crowded sidewalk, arms full of bags stuffed with makeup, hair dye, and lashes. Around her, tents stretched down the block, the smell of cooking oil and city dust heavy in the air. People shuffled past with blankets draped over their shoulders, plastic bags clutched in their hands.

Shirley didn't come with only sandwiches or bottled water, though she carried those, too. She came with something that seemed almost out of place in a setting like this: bright eyeshadow palettes, wigs in bold colors, false lashes.

It was the women on the street who had first asked her to bring makeup to help them feel like themselves again. When Shirley handed one of them a tube of lipstick for the first time, the woman's face lit up, her cracked lips curving into a smile that had been buried under weeks of exhaustion.

"You got purple?" she asked, her voice breaking into laughter.

In that moment, Shirley realized something many had overlooked: homelessness doesn't strip away a person's desire to feel human, to feel beautiful, to look in the mirror and recognize themselves again.

That single encounter stayed with her. She went home, rummaged through her own drawers, and brought back every spare beauty product she had. Soon, friends began donating, and word spread. What started as a few items in a tote bag grew into a nonprofit that would touch thousands: Beauty2TheStreetz.

The organization doesn't just hand out mascara or wigs. Shirley and her team provide hot meals, showers, and hygiene kits alongside hair coloring, makeup application, and hugs. They don't just restore appearances; they restore dignity.

One afternoon, a woman sat in Shirley's folding chair as volunteers washed and conditioned her hair. She closed her eyes and smiled, letting out a soft laugh as the warm water ran through her curls. "It feels so good to be pampered," she said. "I can't remember the last time someone did my hair."

That's the heartbeat of Beauty2TheStreetz. For Shirley, it's never just about lashes or lip gloss. It's about reminding people who feel invisible that they still matter.

The need grew even sharper during the COVID-19 pandemic. Shelters closed, resources dried up, and the streets became more dangerous. While others pulled back, Shirley doubled down. Even when bulk stores limited purchases, even when donations slowed to a trickle, she refused to stop showing up.

"What kind of organization would we be if we only served when it was easy?" she said. And so, with a mask on her face and sanitizer in her pocket, she kept handing out food, supplies, and eyeliner, because for the people she served, it wasn't just about survival. It was about dignity.

Today, Shirley is known as the "mother of Skid Row." She knows names, remembers birthdays, and celebrates every new job interview, every sober milestone, every smile that flickers back to life in her chair.

Her story is proof that kindness isn't about solving everything; it's about showing up, again and again, with open hands and an open heart. Shirley brings Beauty2TheStreetz, one brush stroke, one meal, one act of love at a time.

(MKRO Kindness Grant Winner, Aug 2020)

> **Reflection:** Shirley's work shows that restoring dignity and self-worth is just as vital as meeting physical needs, and that true kindness recognizes the humanity in everyone, no matter their circumstances. How can kindness help bridge differences between people?

It's not what you gather in life, but what you scatter in life, that tells the kind of life you have lived.

– Helen Walton

FROM PATIENT
TO PROVIDER

♥

The hospital room was quiet except for the steady hum of the machines. Sonia Su, just 24 years old, sat curled up on the bed, her body weak from months of chemotherapy. A stack of textbooks sat untouched on the chair beside her, a reminder of the graduate program she paused when her life was suddenly rerouted by an aggressive form of non-Hodgkin's lymphoma.

She had already been through two relapses. By March of 2019, as she faced her final round of treatment, Sonia was beyond exhausted, physically wiped out, emotionally wrung dry, and wrapped in that particular kind of loneliness cancer patients know all too well. The kind that shows up even when people love you.

That day, a nurse entered the room carrying a plain-looking bag. "This was left by someone who's been through treatment," she said softly, setting it on Sonia's tray. Inside were small but thoughtful items: ginger chews to calm nausea, cozy socks, lotion for her sensitive skin, and a handwritten note. Sonia held the letter carefully, her hands trembling as she read the words of encouragement from a stranger who had walked this same brutal road . . . and made it through.

For the first time in weeks, Sonia didn't feel so alone. Somewhere out there was proof that survival was possible, and that someone cared enough to reach back and say, I see you. You've got this.

That one act of kindness changed everything for Sonia. It gave her something her doctors could not prescribe: hope.

When she finally entered remission, she carried that bag and the feeling it gave her, like a compass. She knew she had to pay it forward. In May 2020, Sonia founded Kits to Heart, a nonprofit that delivers cancer care kits to patients and caregivers across the country. What started as a single bag in a quiet hospital room has since rippled outward with the effort of over 9,000 volunteers putting together thousands of kits and bringing comfort, solidarity, and smiles to people in all fifty states.

Each kit is designed with the thoughtfulness that only someone who has lived through treatment could bring. Sonia fills them with items she once clung to: ginger chews, hand sanitizer, soft masks, water bottles, notebooks, and SPF lotion. Volunteers add handmade touches, cards with uplifting words, carefully folded origami, crocheted bags, and friendship bracelets. Together, they turn ordinary boxes into something that feels like a hug you can hold.

Sonia says her goal is simple: to make sure no patient feels the kind of isolation she once felt. "Cancer can be so lonely," she explains. "Sometimes friends and family don't know how to help, and hospitals don't always provide the resources patients really need. A kit is a reminder that someone understands, that you're not fighting alone."

What makes Sonia's story even more remarkable is that she built Kits to Heart while still in the thick of her own recovery, traveling back and forth to regular checkups and scans. Even as her body was healing, her heart was pouring out to others.

Today, hundreds of volunteers have joined Sonia's mission, contributing thousands of hours to write notes, fold origami, and fill boxes with love. Each kit that leaves her hands carries a message of compassion, comfort, and deep solidarity.

Sonia turned her greatest struggle into a wellspring of hope for others. And with every kit that arrives on a hospital bedside, she is paying forward the same gift that once carried her through, the gift of kindness, wrapped in solidarity and love.

(MKRO Kindness Award Winner, Nov 2020)

> **Reflection:** Sonia's dedication shows us that even in the hardest battles, kindness and thoughtful support can light the way and remind us that no one is ever truly alone. What is one small way you can offer comfort or hope to someone going through a difficult time in your community?

*No one cares how much you know
until they know how
much you care.*

– Theodore Roosevelt

SPREADING LITERACY AND JOY

❤

On a spring afternoon in 2017, a stack of donated books sat on a table in a crowded elementary school library. A little boy picked one up, a worn copy of *Where the Wild Things Are,* and held it carefully, almost reverently. "Do I get to keep this?" he asked, eyes wide. When told yes, he hugged it to his chest like he'd just won the lottery.

Seventeen-year-old Agha Haider, the brain and heart behind the book drive, watched the moment unfold. Books had always been a given in his life. His shelves at home were filled with stories. But here was a kid treating a simple paperback as if it were gold. And that moment hit Agha hard. How could something so basic feel so rare? That was the moment Agha realized that thousands of kids in his own community had never owned a book of their own.

That small human moment planted the seed for what would become The Literacy Initiative, a nonprofit Agha founded to put books directly into the hands of children and, more importantly, to let them know they matter.

What started with 2,000 donated books blossomed into a movement reaching across St. Louis, Missouri. But Agha's vision quickly grew beyond handing out books. He saw that reading was not only about words on a page. It was about confidence, belonging, and having someone in your corner. And so, The Literacy Initiative expanded into programs that nurture the whole child: mind, body, and spirit.

Like Books & Cookies, where elementary students meet with high school mentors for icebreakers, reading activities, and, of course, a sweet treat. The room often fills with the sound of laughter as students sound out tricky words or share their favorite parts of a story. Every other week, each child takes home a brand-new book and with it, a growing sense of pride.

And Books & Basketball which offers a similar pairing of mentorship and fun. On the court, kids practice teamwork and resilience. In quiet corners afterward, they read with their high school buddies. These programs, now with around twenty active clubs, are helping young students discover not only the joy of reading but the steady presence of someone cheering them on.

The impact has been remarkable. Airport Elementary School, once at the bottom of its district in reading scores, leapt forward after partnering with The Literacy Initiative. Principal Staci Wallington remembers watching Agha's work unfold. "I observed a real-life hero," she said. "He was young, but driven. He provided books for homes, school supplies for students, and tutors who believed in them. He did it all with a smile."

When COVID-19 threatened to halt everything, Agha refused to let the momentum die. He launched online one-on-one tutoring and created eCamp, a summer program where high school volunteers designed and taught classes on everything from creative writing to coding. Over one hundred unique sessions brought joy and learning into children's homes during months of uncertainty.

The Literacy Initiative proves that kindness ripples outward in unexpected ways. It began with a teenager watching a boy clutch his very first book. Today, it's a network of students lifting one another up with stories, with mentorship, and with love.

At its heart, Agha's story is about the power of noticing. He noticed a problem: children growing up without the basic building blocks of literacy. And instead of walking away, he leaned in with compassion, determination, and vision. One kindness at a time, he's showing that young people don't have to wait to change the world. They can start now with a book, a smile, and the belief that every child deserves both.

(MKRO Kindness Award Winner, Nov 2020)

> **Reflection:** Agha's dedication reminds us that empowering young minds through literacy and mentorship not only changes individual lives but also strengthens entire communities. What's one act of kindness you'll never forget, and why?

*I've been looking for a way
to heal myself, and I've found
that kindness is the best way.*

– Lady Gaga

KINDNESS IN MOTION

The air was sharp that afternoon, the kind of cold that bites at your fingers and makes you tuck your chin into your coat. Marina Arias, then just fourteen, was walking with her mom when they noticed a teenage boy sitting on the sidewalk. He was hunched over, arms wrapped tight, no coat, no protection from the Northern Humboldt winter. He looked cold in a way that went way past temperature, tired, worn down, and very much alone.

Marina's mom stopped. She didn't look away, the way so many of us might when faced with suffering we don't know how to fix. Instead, she dug into her pocket. All she had was five dollars. It wasn't much, certainly not enough to solve the boy's problems, but it was something. She pressed the bill into his hand.

Back at home, the image of that boy lingered. "We can do more," Marina's mom said. She turned to Marina and her sister, and together they scoured their small house. They gathered what they could: a blanket, canned food, a hat, spare change, masks, sanitizer, even dog food, apologizing to their own pup, Diesel, as his kibble was scooped into a bag. Marina added her favorite grey sweatshirt, a piece of clothing she loved but knew someone else needed more.

When they returned to the boy, the gratitude in his eyes said more than words could. Marina remembers the way her mom gently told him about a local shelter and wished him warmth and safety. At that moment, the giving of not just things but dignity imprinted itself deeply on Marina's heart.

It was more than a single act of kindness. It was the spark of a mission.

Soon after, Marina began creating Kindness Kits for people experiencing homelessness in her community. Each kit is practical and thoughtful: hats, gloves, socks, blankets, protein-rich food with easy-open lids, water, snacks, and dog treats. Nestled among the supplies is always a handwritten note: You are loved. Each one also includes a list of local resources for food, shelter, and support.

She and her mom keep the kits in their car, ready to hand out whenever they meet someone in need. And here's the thing, this hasn't been easy. Marina's family faces financial struggles of their own, and her mom, a disabled single mother and former nurse, is preparing for ankle surgery. Still, they stretch what little they have. Marina earns money for supplies through chores, while her mom sometimes contributes by using credit. Through it all, her mother repeats the words that guide their family: I am blessed, I am equipped, and I have the favor of God.

Marina has taken that wisdom to heart. "There are a lot of drifters and regulars in our area with little help," she wrote in her grant application. "If you feel down, just look around and do for others! You will realize how truly blessed you are."

She's right. Kindness doesn't require a full bank account or a perfect plan. It only asks us to notice, to really see another person's humanity, and to do *something*. Marina's Kindness Kits are more than supplies in a bag. They're a lifeline, a reminder of dignity, a message of hope.

And it all began on a cold day, with a mother and daughter refusing to walk past a sad-looking boy.

(MKRO Kindness Grant Winner, Feb 2021)

Reflection: Marina's story reminds us that compassion doesn't require wealth, just willingness. How do you want people to feel after they've interacted with you?

Kindness begins with the understanding that we all struggle.

– Charles Glassman

BAKING A BETTER WORLD

♥

The kitchen was quiet in a way it had never been before. For thirteen-year-old Nigel Mushambi, that silence was unsettling. Just weeks earlier, he and his older brother Shane had spent hours there, kneading dough, laughing at their own messes, and delivering sweet treats through their little business, 2 Bros In The Kitchen. Now, thanks to the pandemic, the oven sat cold, and the mixing bowls stacked neatly on the counter seemed like relics of a different world.

Schools had shut down. His homeschool co-op had moved online. The baking business he loved was paused. Nigel was restless, frustrated, and like so many kids his age, unsure of how to make sense of the strange, empty days.

One afternoon, as he sat slumped at the table in full what-is-my-life mode, his mom looked at him thoughtfully and asked a question that would change everything: "What are you going to tell your grandchildren you did during the lockdown?"

The question landed with unexpected weight. Nigel had been thinking only about what he had lost: friends, routines, business opportunities, freedom. But suddenly, he realized something big: this was history. And he had a choice: let the days slip by, or use them to do something that mattered.

That night, Nigel's mind kept circling back to his teachers. He thought about the sudden way their lives had been upended, too, how they were juggling Zoom classes, worrying about their students, and carrying their own fears about the virus. They showed up anyway. "They're working so hard," he thought, "and who's saying thank you?"

The answer came to him the way all of his best ideas did, in the kitchen. Flour. Sugar. Butter. Cookies. Not just treats, but little packages of gratitude.

He set himself a goal that felt impossibly big and slightly unhinged: one thousand cookies for one thousand teachers. A thousand small reminders that their work mattered.

And just like that, the Mushambi kitchen came back to life. The whir of the mixer replaced the silence. The sweet smell of chocolate chip dough baking filled the air. With each tray that came out of the oven, Nigel wasn't just baking, he was sending a message: You're seen. You're appreciated. You're not alone in this hard moment.

The response from teachers said it all. Smiles. Tears. Notes of thanks that proved something important: kindness doesn't need to be complicated. Sometimes, it's just a warm cookie showing up at exactly the right moment.

Of course, baking was nothing new for Nigel and Shane. They'd been in the kitchen since they were toddlers, and after winning a local baking competition three years in a row, they turned their passion into 2 Bros In The Kitchen. But from the beginning, it was never just about desserts. As Nigel likes to say, "We don't just want a world with happy taste buds. We want people to have happy stomachs and hearts, too."

And they've lived that mission in countless ways: providing meals for the homeless, donating toys to children, raising funds for medical care, handing out frozen pops to unhoused neighbors, delivering cake-in-a-jar treats to police officers and community leaders, and distributing school supplies to kids in need.

But in 2020, when the world felt upside down, Nigel found his clearest answer yet to his mom's question. He would tell his grandchildren that when the world shut down, he chose kindness. He chose to fill ovens, fill boxes, and fill hearts.

Because sometimes, in the darkest seasons, a simple cookie can carry a whole lot of hope.

(MKRO Kindness Grant Winner, Feb 2021)

> **Reflection:** Nigel's story reminds us that even during challenging times, generosity and creativity can turn small acts into powerful expressions of kindness and gratitude. How can acts of kindness help us cope with personal challenges or grief?

We can't help everyone, but everyone can help someone.

– Ronald Reagan

EMBRACING IDENTITY

When Nicole Munoz was sixteen, she sat in the corner of a hospital waiting room, watching a girl about her age twist her hoodie strings around her fingers. The girl's eyes were red, her shoulders hunched like she was trying to disappear into herself. Nicole didn't know her story, but she didn't need to. She had seen that look before, in friends, in classmates, in the mirror. It's the look of someone carrying a heavy battle on the inside, afraid that no one would understand.

Nicole had already volunteered more than two hundred hours in healthcare settings, enough time to see how mental health struggles can shadow young people's lives. Again and again, she noticed the same pattern: what made the struggle heavier wasn't just the depression, or the anxiety, or the confusion about identity. It was the silence. The feeling of being unseen, unheard, or worse, judged.

She thought about her own peers: teens trying to figure out who they were, trying on pieces of identity like clothes that didn't always fit. It was a tender, vulnerable time of life, and yet so many were met with skepticism or rejection instead of encouragement. Nicole knew how damaging that lack of acceptance could be. She also knew it didn't have to be that way.

That summer of 2020, while the world seemed to stop, Nicole decided she couldn't sit still. With her notebooks spread across the kitchen table, she sketched out an idea: what if there was a place where young people could speak openly about who they were, and instead of judgment, they were met with curiosity and respect? What if there was a platform where voices often pushed to the margins could be heard and valued?

Six months of late nights, research, and planning later, her vision became real. She launched Positive I, an organization dedicated to helping youth embrace the facets of their identity that make them unique. Its mission was simple but profound: to cultivate understanding, so that no teen would have to feel invisible or unloved simply for being themselves.

Her first step was a podcast. Nicole invited young people to share their stories, what it was like to grow up navigating race, gender, culture, sexuality, and all the layers of identity that shaped them. The first time she hit "record," she felt a mix of nerves and hope. But then the guest began to speak, and something shifted. Here was a voice, trembling but brave, saying out loud what had so often been silenced.

Listeners began writing in. Some said the podcast made them feel less alone. Others admitted it had opened their eyes to struggles they hadn't understood before. Nicole realized she had created more than a podcast; she had created a bridge. A way for people to cross into one another's stories, to see humanity before making assumptions.

Nicole's dream is as bold as it is beautiful: a society where young people can stand fully in who they are without fear of rejection. A world where understanding comes before judgment, and acceptance is the norm, not the exception.

The waiting room girl might never hear Nicole's podcast. But thousands of others will. And in their quietest moments when they most need a reminder that they are worthy of love and belonging, Nicole's work will be there, gently reminding them of the truth: you matter, just as you are.

(MKRO Kindness Award Winner, May 2021)

Reflection: Nicole's dedication teaches us that embracing and understanding our unique identities is essential to fostering acceptance, empathy, and mental well-being for ourselves and others. What has helping others taught you about resilience?

Unexpected kindness is the most powerful, least costly, and most underrated agent of human change.

– Bob Kerrey

FROM WALL STREET TO THE OCEAN FLOOR

When Mike Goldberg took a group of divers down to a reef in the Florida Keys, he remembers the silence. Not the usual peaceful quiet of being underwater, but a hollow stillness, no darting schools of fish, no colors pulsing from coral, just a graveyard of bleached white skeletons. Mike felt an ache in his chest. He had seen it too many times: reefs that once burst with color and sound now reduced to barren rock.

Mike hadn't started out as a reef protector. For years, he sat behind a desk in financial services, chasing numbers that never seemed to fill the void. "I felt like I was just chasing money," he admitted, "but not being true to my core." Eventually, the pull of the ocean became too strong to ignore. He left that world behind, moved his family to Islamorada in the Florida Keys, and opened a small dive shop called Key Dives.

With over 10,000 dives to his name, Mike had swum with humpback whales, marveled at tiny, jewel-colored nudibranchs, and once floated above a reef so alive it looked like fireworks under the sea. But he had also watched that same reef decline year after year, until it no longer resembled the place he first fell in love with. Coral disease, rising water temperatures, and human activity left devastation in their wake.

Mike could have turned away. He could have accepted that this was the cost of climate change, that ordinary people couldn't possibly make a difference. Instead, he asked: What if we tried?

Together with marine biologist Dr. Kylie Smith, Mike co-founded I.CARE: (Islamorada Conservation and Restoration Education). Their idea was simple but radical: don't leave reef restoration only to scientists. Invite the community to help. Their mission was, among other things, to train recreational divers to plant nursery-grown coral, monitor its growth, and clear away threats like marine debris and invasive species. Hand ordinary people a fragment of coral and say, "Here. Plant this. You are part of the healing."

The impact was immediate. Divers who once came to the Keys seeking adventure now left with something deeper: a sense of purpose. Mike remembers one teenager who planted her first coral fragment and surfaced beaming. "I feel like I just put life back into the ocean," she said. That small act, hands trembling with care as she pressed living coral into rock, was a gesture of hope.

Today, I.CARE has restored tens of thousands of corals and educated and trained over 4,000 volunteers. Schoolchildren suit up for their first dives and come face-to-face with the fragile ecosystems they're helping to protect. Families return year after year, not just to vacation, but to check on reefs they helped plant. They aren't tourists anymore; they're caretakers.

Mike says the work is about more than numbers. "Every coral we plant is a story," he explains. "It's someone deciding that the ocean matters enough to save."

His own story is proof. He walked away from a life that didn't feel true, chose passion over profit, and built something that gives people not only a way to heal the ocean but also a way to heal themselves. Because when you take part in bringing a reef back to life, you don't just see hope, you plant it.

(MKRO Kindness Grant Winner, Jan 2025)

> **Reflection:** Mike's vision proves that protecting our planet is most powerful when communities come together. What's one small way you can help restore or protect the natural spaces around you?

*Measure what matters,
not just what you can count.*

– Jacqueline Novogratz

CASTING HOPE

On a warm summer morning in Washington, D.C., a group of kids stood on the edge of the Anacostia River, fishing rods in hand. For most of them, it was the first time they'd ever seen the water this close, the first time they'd been invited to slow down, breathe, and hope for a tug on the line. One boy, about twelve years old, stared out across the rippling surface and whispered to Carmen Garner, "I didn't even know this existed." Carmen smiled because he knew that feeling. He'd been that kid, the one who thought the world was dangerous, small, and definitely not built for dreaming.

Carmen is the founder of Inner City Anglers, a nonprofit born from something simple yet profound: kindness. During the pandemic, when stimulus checks landed in mailboxes across the country, Carmen made a bold choice. Instead of saving it or paying bills, he would use his check as seed money to start a program that would give inner-city kids the same thing that once saved his own life; fishing.

Growing up, Carmen's life was anything but easy. His mother died of AIDS when he was young. He moved through seventeen different relatives' homes before he was old enough to be on his own. Stepping outside often meant stepping into real danger. "People get shot out there. People get killed out there," he recalls. But there was one bright spot: his cousin's boyfriend took him fishing. Standing by the water, line cast, Carmen felt something he hadn't known before: Safety. Possibility. Peace. That man's quiet gesture of kindness became an anchor for a boy who desperately needed one.

Years later, as a teacher and mentor, Carmen knew he had to pay that gift forward. "Fishing saved my life," he says simply. "Now, it's my turn to save theirs."

Through Inner City Anglers, Carmen does far more than teach kids how to catch fish. He teaches them self-worth, perseverance, and resilience. Every cast becomes a lesson: about reaching out, taking a chance, and trusting that what you put into the world can come back to you. He calls it "casting dreams into reality."

One boy's story stays with him. Carmen asked the child what he would do if someone insulted his mother. The boy's face hardened: "I would kill them." It was raw, angry, and real. Six weeks later, after fishing trips, long talks, and lessons in self-reflection, Carmen asked again. This time, the boy paused before saying, "I got too much to lose to let another person determine my actions."

That shift had nothing to do with fishing and everything to do with being seen. Someone believed in him, and that belief changed how he saw himself.

That's Carmen's mission. To show kids who have been told all their lives *you can't*, that actually, *yeah, you can*. That they are more than their zip code, their losses, or their fears.

Every child who steps onto the riverbank with Carmen is offered more than a rod and reel. They are offered dignity, hope, and the reminder that kindness has the power to ripple outward in ways we can't measure.

Carmen's life proves that a single act of generosity, one man taking a scared kid fishing, can echo decades later in the lives of countless children. Because of him, the next generation of inner-city kids will cast not just for fish, but for futures they never thought possible.

(MKRO Kindness Award Winner, May 2021)

Reflection: Carmen's story reminds us that mentorship and hope can change the trajectory of a young person's life, showing them their worth and limitless potential. In what ways has kindness shaped who you are today?

One message, at just the right moment, can change someone's entire day, outlook or life.

– Megan Murphy

A VOICE FOR THE PLANET

❤

At just ten years old, Sarah Goody's world felt unbearably heavy. The sadness came in waves, sometimes so overwhelming that she couldn't imagine ever feeling light again. She had been diagnosed with clinical depression, and for years, she carried the invisible weight of loneliness and despair. Nights dragged on. Days blurred together. She often wondered if she'd ever find her way back to joy.

Then, something shifted. In the middle of her darkest chapter, Sarah stumbled into activism. Not in some dramatic movie-montage way, more like reading, listening, paying attention, and slowly realizing the world was on fire (sometimes literally). What started as curiosity turned into purpose. "I think it saved me," Sarah says. "Activism gave me something to look forward to, something bigger than my own sadness."

The first time she went to a climate rally, she remembers standing shoulder to shoulder with other young people holding signs, their voices rose together, loud and determined. And for the first time in a long time, Sarah didn't feel invisible. She didn't feel powerless. She felt like she belonged to something bigger.

That moment changed everything. The quiet, hurting kid became a leader with a voice, strong enough to move crowds. At sixteen, Sarah founded Climate Now, a youth-led organization focused on educating and mobilizing kids to fight climate change. In classrooms and community centers, Sarah stood in front of her peers, sometimes trembling, always determined, sharing her story and urging others to take action. She told them what she wished someone had told her years earlier: you matter, and your voice absolutely counts.

Her activism didn't stop there. Through her second project, Broadway Speaks Up, she convinced performers from more than fifty Broadway shows to use their platforms to talk about climate awareness. Watching artists, she once admired on stage, speak out about environmental justice because she asked them to, it was a moment of awe. It was proof that one young person's courage could ripple outward in ways she had never imagined.

And even when the pandemic shut down much of the world, Sarah didn't pause. Instead, she volunteered over 700 hours at the Three Ring Ranch Exotic Animal Sanctuary in Hawaii. Each morning, she rose early to feed ostriches, clean enclosures, or comfort monkeys and zebras. Caring for those animals, Sarah said, reminded her of the fragile beauty of the earth, and why protecting it matters so deeply.

What makes Sarah's story so powerful isn't just the activism itself. It's the transformation. The way she turned her pain into purpose. The lonely little girl who once wondered if she'd ever feel hope again became the young woman standing at podiums, on stages, and in classrooms telling others: *"Your voice is powerful. So use it."*

Sarah's journey is a reminder that change often begins in the quietest, most broken places. By choosing action over despair, she not only healed herself, but inspired countless others to believe they could do the same. Her kindness isn't soft or small; it's fierce, determined, and unstoppable. And like the rallies where she first found her voice, Sarah's story echoes with a promise: when one person dares to care deeply, it can awaken a movement that touches the world.

(MKRO Kindness Award Winner, May 2021)

> **Reflection:** Sarah's story reminds us that turning personal challenges into meaningful activism can spark hope, healing, and real change, no matter how young or where we start. Imagine you could start a movement, just like Sarah did. What would you want to change? Who would you want to help? Share your ideas with someone close to you.

This is your reminder to savor everything in your life, no matter how mundane or familiar. Because you never know when you'll experience something for the very last time.

– Sam Harris

FROM HUNGER
TO HOPE

❤

One rainy morning in Mansfield, Connecticut, Humza Zaida pulled up behind the Holy Family Home & Shelter with his car loaded to the brim with trays of fresh food, pasta, roasted vegetables, and loaves of bread still warm from the oven. As he and his volunteers carried the meals inside, a little boy peeked out from behind his mother's legs. His eyes widened at the sight of the food, his face lighting up with wonder and relief. In that moment, the shelter felt a little less like a shelter and a lot more like home.

That small moment stuck with Humza. For that boy, dinner that night wasn't just calories on a plate; it was dignity, warmth, and the rare feeling of being cared for. Humza knew that feeling all too well. Growing up in a food-insecure household, he remembered the nights when his own family had to stretch cans of soup or quietly skip meals. Hunger wasn't an abstract issue he read about; it was personal. Later, while attending the University of Connecticut, he realized many of his classmates were quietly fighting the same battle, they just didn't talk about it. They smiled, showed up to class, and pretended they weren't hungry.

At first, Humza joined the campus SOS Food Recovery program, helping to recycle unused student dining hall swipes. But the more he learned, the clearer the problem became: there wasn't a food shortage, there was a waste problem. Perfectly good food was being thrown out while families just a few miles away were going hungry.

That realization lit a fire in him. If food was being wasted, why couldn't it be redirected? Why couldn't the "extra" become someone's lifeline?

So Humza launched the Restaurant Resource Project, a community-powered initiative that partners with a dozen local restaurants. Each day, he and more than forty volunteers rescue untouched, perfectly good food, items that would otherwise be thrown out because of over-ordering or storage limits. Instead of filling dumpsters, those meals fill plates at shelters and soup kitchens like Covenant Soup Kitchen, where families know the food is fresh, nourishing, and made with care.

Was it easy? Of course not. Moving hot food safely required thermal blankets, coolers, scales, and careful coordination. But Humza never let the obstacles dim his determination. "Food insecurity isn't always about scarcity," he explains. "It's about distribution." And he decided to be the bridge.

The impact goes far beyond numbers. Each delivery is a reminder to families that they are not invisible. Parents can sit down to dinner with their kids without the crushing stress of wondering where the next meal will come from. Volunteers see the relief on people's faces when they realize tonight, at least, they don't have to choose between groceries and rent.

Humza has taken one of the hardest parts of his own child-hood and flipped the script. Where once he felt the ache of an empty plate, now he fills them. Where he once felt powerless, now he empowers.

The Restaurant Resource Project isn't just feeding stomachs, it's feeding futures. Each rescued tray of food is also a message: you matter, you are cared for, and you are not forgotten.

Through his work, Humza reminds us of something profound: that sometimes the most ordinary acts, delivering a meal, saving what others overlook, can ripple outward in extraordinary ways.

(MKRO Kindness Grant Winner, Aug 2021)

Reflection: Humza's journey shows us that compassion and initiative can transform personal hardship into lasting hope for others. What role does empathy play in your idea of kindness?

When we value connections and kindness over material wealth, then our human spirit soars.

– Unknown

EIGHTEEN ACTS, ENDLESS IMPACT

This Kindness Hero chose to remain anonymous, but her story is included here exactly as it happened, because the impact of her kindness deserves to be shared. Shai Mankin is a pseudonym.

Shai Mankin proves that there's no such thing as a small act of kindness. For her, spreading kindness isn't about waiting for a big opportunity; it's about finding little ways every day to brighten someone else's life.

Whether through volunteering, smiling at a stranger, or quietly slipping a dessert into a customer's order during her shifts at a fast-food job, Shai made kindness her daily practice.

Shai said, "I've always wanted to make a difference in the lives of others, and this led me to my career choice of nursing. I'm starting my second year of university. I still do strive to have a positive impact, but I also realize it's never too early to find ways to do so and that even the little things make a difference. Holding the door open, asking someone how their day went, or just smiling at someone can make a difference."

That philosophy guided her through countless small but meaningful acts, volunteering at community events, creating candy sleighs with her cousins to deliver to first responders, and finding creative ways to bring joy in unexpected places.

For Shai, no gesture is too small if it makes someone feel seen.

When Shai turned eighteen, she wanted to celebrate in a way that reflected her values. Instead of a traditional party, she applied for our grant with a unique idea: to spend her birthday completing 18 random acts of kindness, one for each year of her life.

Her list of ideas was both simple and deeply thoughtful:

- Giving flower bouquets to hospital nurses to pass along to patients in need of cheer
- Delivering chocolates and handwritten notes to nursing home residents
- Bringing cupcakes to Hope Cottage, a shelter for women and children
- Leaving coins in laundry rooms and parking meters
- Paying for someone's coffee or food
- Surprising passersby with $5 gift cards and kind messages
- Placing dollar bills near items at the dollar store to surprise people
- Distributing snack bags to first responders and fellow students

Some plans went even further, like gifting toys to a child who might otherwise go without a birthday present, preparing a full meal for a family in need, assembling care packages for homeless individuals, or handing out stuffed animals to children at pediatric hospitals. Every gesture would include an encouraging note, a reminder that kindness exists in the world.

"I truly believe kindness makes a huge difference," Shai shared. "I would love to celebrate life by brightening the lives of others."

Her birthday wish is not just about performing good deeds; it's about sparking a ripple effect of positivity. Each act invites recipients to not only feel joy, but to pay that feeling forward, making compassion contagious.

We were honored to help Shai bring her birthday dream to life. Her creative and heartfelt plan embodies the spirit of the MKRO family, showing us that age is no barrier to impact. Shai reminds us all that the best way to celebrate life is by lifting others up.

Happy birthday, Shai, and thank you for proving that small acts can create extraordinary ripples.

(MKRO Kindness Grant Winner, Aug 2021)

Reflection: Shai's journey reminds us that kindness often begins with listening to people's real needs. How do you lead with kindness in your life?

AND THEN CAME THE RIPPLES

❤

(Part 2 of Shai's story.)

What Shai Mankin set in motion on her eighteenth birthday didn't end with a plan, it unfolded into moments, smiles, and connections that stretched far beyond a single day. After her birthday of kindness, Shai sent us a letter describing how those eighteen acts came to life. Her letter, brimming with excitement and gratitude, left us smiling all day. We couldn't wait to share it, so others could feel that joy and perhaps pass it along in their own ways, too.

Hi to everyone at MKRO,

I want to start off by thanking you for choosing to help fund my idea and for all your support. I had been thinking about this idea since May, at which time I did not think I would be able to do everything I wanted to do. When I found out I was chosen, I couldn't believe it, and I was so excited. I'm not exaggerating when

I say that the moments spent planning for and implementing these different ways of spreading kindness have been some of the best and most exciting moments of my entire life.

I started a countdown on my whiteboard days before, and I was constantly talking about it with my roommate and adjusting ideas when we thought of new things.

Again, to be able to put this idea into action was such a blessing, and it was literally a dream come true for me. Thank you, tons!

Here are some of the things I did with my roommates' help.

We started off by leaving snacks in the laundry room, along with some note cards with motivational quotes. We had also planned to leave change for the machines, but laundry is free this year!

A couple of weeks ago, I started listening to a book called The Compound Effect and loved it, so I bought a copy, put a Starbucks gift card inside, wrapped it up, and placed it on some tables outside of Starbucks. Although we don't know who took it, when we passed by around 20 minutes later, it was gone!

Then, we headed out to find some vending machines to attach a notecard with money for a snack/drink.

We then loaded up and headed into town to spread some more kindness! Our first stop was Dollar Tree, where we left some dollars and bought some things we still needed.

Our plan for the park was to leave some toys with a note for whoever found them to keep. When we were walking to find a place to leave the soccer ball, this cute kid started pointing at it and saying something like "play," and his mom kept telling him it wasn't his. We just had to give it to him. He was so excited and wouldn't stop looking at it while he held it! It was one of the best parts of my day!

When we gave out one of the gift cards at the park, a lady was a little skeptical at first and asked if there were no strings attached and if we were sure. She finally took it happily and said she was from out of town and would be sure to use it before she left.

We also took a gift to a nursing center and asked the worker to give it to someone they thought needed it most. In it were slippers, a big warm blanket, mug cake packets, a coffee mug, and a bag of Hershey's kisses. We hope it brightened someone's day!

At Walmart, we estimated the cost of the groceries of the person behind us and bought a gift card to cover the cost. I handed it to the lady behind us right before leaving.

Another of our stops was at the hospital, where we dropped off some bouquets of flowers for patients, different toys for kids, and a basket with snacks and candy for the workers. The nurse from the ER department was very appreciative and said it was a great way to end the day.

Along the way, we also gave out the baggies we put together for the homeless. In them were a travel-size lotion and body wash, wipes, deodorant, a couple of packs of snacks, socks, and a shirt.

We also made a stop by the Hope Cottage, a homeless shelter for women and children. I had called in advance to obtain an age range for a child who had a recent birthday, and we were able to deliver a birthday present based on what she liked (Frozen pajamas, stickers, a Paw Patrol toy, a small chocolate cake, some chocolates, and a tray of cookies). She immediately grabbed the bag, said thank you, and started walking away; I think she liked it.

Our last stop was the police station, where we dropped off some snacks and a gift.

I feel like I could go on forever. There are also a few more we couldn't get to (like the drive-thru we chose to pay for someone's food in, where we waited and waited and no one got in line behind us, so we left and tried another one, in which there was a problem at the register so we decided to buy a gift card to go to the next person's order but they were out of them.

We will finish the remaining this weekend; I can't wait!

Thank you so much again for making what was once a dream a reality. It is a blessing to be able to brighten others' days, and these are all moments I will cherish forever. I hope that you all are happy with how this turned out, too, and I can't thank you all enough for your help. Matt's kindness will ripple on forever.

Sincerely,

Shai

After reading Shai's letter, it's impossible not to feel inspired. Her creative acts of kindness weren't grand or flashy; they were thoughtful, heartfelt, and deeply meaningful. And they remind us that kindness doesn't need a special occasion to matter.

We love the idea of celebrating a birthday with a kindness campaign, but really, any day can be a kindness day. It doesn't have to cost money, either. Imagine setting a goal to do 10 kind acts in a day: smiling at 10 people, giving 10 compliments, thanking 10 workers, or leaving 10 uplifting notes in random places. Small actions, big feelings. Make a day of it and you'll find it makes you feel good too.

Thank you, Shai, for your joy, compassion, and creativity. You've shown us how contagious kindness truly is.

Happy 18th. The world is brighter because of you.

(MKRO Kindness Grant Winner, Aug 2021)

> **Reflection:** Shai reminds us of the pure joy that kindness can bring. What simple act of kindness do you enjoy doing?

Just because you're happy doesn't mean that the day is perfect, but that you have looked beyond its imperfections.

– Bob Marley

THE ROAD TO KINDNESS

It was a sweltering July afternoon in Temple, Texas, when Liz Buechele walked into a hospital lobby carrying a box of cake pops. Nurses and doctors, weary from long shifts, paused as she offered them a sweet treat with a smile and a simple thank you. Down the hall, she handed confetti poppers to patients, who lit up with laughter as the tiny explosions filled the sterile corridors with bursts of color. Just like that, the air shifted, tired faces softened, laughter echoed, and a really hard day got a little lighter.

Moments like this are the heartbeat of Liz's work.

Liz, who lived in New York City, never set out to lead a movement. It all started back in 2011, as a high school senior in Western Pennsylvania. One unseasonably warm day, she was driving home with the windows down, radio up, feeling invincible in that very specific seventeen-year-old way, when a thought popped into her head:

"Day 1: Happiness is... those perfect car rides where the radio just plays all the right songs."

Like any seventeen-year-old in 2011 who thought they had a world-changing idea, she went home and posted it on Facebook. And then she posted again the next day. And the next. Over time, what began as a simple daily gratitude post turned into a personal commitment - now more than 5,000 daily joys shared.

That moment was what Liz now calls her "aha moment," the spark that would ignite something much bigger than a social media habit. She realized happiness didn't have to be rare or complicated, and kindness didn't have to be grand to be powerful. What if, she wondered, we practiced it daily? What if it became a way of life?

And so, The Smile Project was born, a nonprofit dedicated to spreading happiness through daily kindness, gratitude practices, and youth service clubs. The mission was simple but profound: help people slow down, notice one another, and discover the joy that comes from giving.

But Liz doesn't just talk about kindness, she out there doing it. In 2018, she launched the Kindness Always Tour, a fifty-six day journey across the United States to spark chain reactions of generosity. At every stop, she partnered with strangers, students, and community groups to carry out projects that rippled outward.

In Cleveland, a group of Girl Scouts crafted cheerful gift baskets and sent them with Liz to Savannah, Georgia. From there, Liz delivered the baskets to Fur Kids Animal Shelter in Atlanta, where new puppy parents were surprised with a bundle of supplies and love. In Charleston, South Carolina, she bought travel mugs at a local coffee shop, leaving them behind for the next customers, no **big** announcement, just surprise kindness with caffeine.

Each act was small on its own, but together they wove a story of connection across the country. Everywhere Liz went, she saw the same thing: people hungry for kindness. Sometimes it showed up as a nurse's tearful gratitude after a grueling shift, sometimes a child's delighted laughter in a shelter, sometimes simply the pause of a stranger realizing they had just been seen.

Beyond her tour, Liz has poured her energy into cultivating young kindness leaders through SPARK Clubs (Strengthening Positivity and Reinforcing Kindness) in high schools and colleges. These student-led groups organize local service projects, bringing the values of empathy and generosity into classrooms, cafeterias, and communities. By mentoring these students, Liz ensures that the ripple of kindness doesn't end with her it multiplies, carried forward by the next generation.

What makes Liz remarkable is not just her creativity and energy but her unwavering belief that kindness is not an accessory to life; it's essential. It can transform a mood, a moment, even a life.

From one warm drive home in 2011 to a nationwide movement, Liz has shown that kindness is contagious, and wildly powerful. She reminds us that no gesture is too small and no person too ordinary to spark joy.

Because when kindness becomes a daily practice, it stops being just a good idea. It becomes a quiet-joyful revolution.

(MKRO Kindness Award Winner, May 2019)

Reflection: Liz's journey reveals how one person's commitment to daily kindness can spark a movement, encouraging gratitude, joy, and service. How could you make kindness a daily habit?

*You don't get to choose how you're
going to die. Or when.
You can only decide how
you're going to live.*

– Joan Baez

FROM ISOLATION TO INCLUSION

When Sriya Tallapragada walked into a math competition as a young teen, she immediately noticed something that made her stomach drop: of the twenty students in the room, she was the only girl. The absence was so loud, she could feel it pressing on her. The boys clustered together, swapping notes and jokes, while she sat quietly, trying to shake off the gnawing thought that she didn't belong. That moment stayed with her. Not as a one-time awkward memory, but as a flashing neon sign pointing to a much bigger issue: girls who love science and math often don't see themselves reflected in those spaces. And when you don't see yourself, it's easy to believe you don't belong, even when you absolutely do.

Then 2020 happened. Schools shut down, the world paused, and fourteen-year-old Sriya found herself with something rare: time. Time to think about that math competition. Time to reflect on the loneliness she felt as a girl who loved STEM (Science, Technology, Engineering, Math). And time to wonder: what if she could change that feeling for someone else? Armed with only her computer, she sat down at her desk and began coding a simple website. She called it Girls Who STEAM – adding the A for Art, because creativity belongs here too.

"I didn't know if anyone would even notice," she admitted. "I crossed my fingers that maybe a few people would join."

Spoiler alert: people noticed.

Within months, her inbox was overflowing with messages from girls across the country, and even around the world, who were hungry for exactly what she was building: a place to learn, connect, and not feel like the only one in the room.

Soon, Girls Who STEAM had grown into a global community with over one hundred volunteers and thousands of participants attending online workshops. One of the most powerful moments came during their teen pitch competition, at the organization's GirlsWithGoals2021 virtual conference. Hundreds of young women logged on to present their startup ideas tackling issues close to their hearts.

One team pitched a bilingual children's book series to help immigrant kids feel seen in classrooms. Another proposed a digital resource hub for mothers juggling work and childcare. The "winners" left with prizes, but the real victory was something bigger; every girl walked away with confidence, feedback, and the rare experience of being taken seriously.

Sriya watched it all with tears in her eyes. "I kept thinking, this is what I wished I had. A space where being a girl in STEM isn't an exception, it's the norm."

Her work didn't stop online. In 2021, as pandemic restrictions eased, Girls Who STEAM launched in-person chapters, ten across the U.S. and more than fifteen internationally. Many of these serve low-income communities, bringing laptops, mentorship, and hands-on workshops to girls who might otherwise never get the chance to explore STEM.

At the heart of it all is still that quiet moment at the math competition, one girl, one desk, one feeling of being out of place. Except now, because Sriya chose to do something about it, thousands of girls are walking into classrooms, conferences, and competitions knowing they belong.

Sriya is living proof that you're never too young to take your pain, turn it into purpose, and change the world. Her story is not just about coding a website; it's about rewriting the narrative for girls everywhere, one act of courage, one community, and one spark of kindness at a time.

(MKRO Kindness Award Winner, Nov 2021)

> **Reflection:** Sriya's story proves that a spark of passion and a drive for equality can empower thousands. What does being a "kindness hero" look like in your own life?

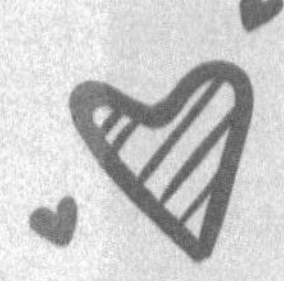

We make a living by what we get.
We make a life by what we give.

– Winston Churchill

WHAT'S YOUR 50?

On a cold January afternoon, Kristen Weinberg stood in a park in Washington, D.C., her arms full of coats and blankets. She and a few friends walked slowly among a group of unhoused neighbors gathered near the benches, handing out warm clothing to people whose smiles said more than words ever could. One man pulled on a thick winter coat and wrapped a scarf around his neck, his face softening and he visibly exhaled - the kind of relief that tells you warmth isn't a luxury, it's a lifeline. Kristen had to blink back tears. Right there, she realized that her small birthday wish had become something much bigger.

Kristen had just turned fifty, and instead of throwing a party or asking for gifts, she wanted to give back. Her idea was simple but powerful: donate fifty items every month for a year to twelve different charities. She called it What's Your 50? It was meant to be a personal project, but as soon as she invited her community to join in, it took on a life of its own.

Her husband was the first to get involved, rallying coworkers to donate socks to the Men's Emergency Shelter in Rockville, Maryland. Socks may seem like an ordinary thing, but they're one of the most requested and least donated items at shelters. Kristen's original goal was fifty pairs. The final tally? Three hundred forty-four.

Friends joined in, too. One organized a drive for I Support the Girls, a nonprofit that provides bras and feminine hygiene products for women in need. Instead of fifty items, one hundred sixty-one came in. Kristen's neighbors' children, eager to help, decided to take on a food drive for Nourish Now, which redistributes surplus groceries to hungry families. They set out to collect fifty jars of peanut butter. The kids went door-to-door, explaining to people why peanut butter mattered so much for food banks. They didn't just reach their goal, they doubled it, collecting one hundred and two jars. Overachievers, all of them.

It seemed everywhere Kristen turned, people were saying yes. The simplicity of the challenge, just fifty of something, made kindness accessible. Big enough to matter, small enough to feel doable. And the results far exceeded anything she imagined.

Within the first month, Kristen wrote on Facebook: "Ok, so you're not going to believe this, but I set a goal exactly one month ago today to collect 50 items for 12 different charities = 600 donations. Not only did you all come through for me, but you SURPASSED my WILDEST dreams!! You have all stepped up and donated over 1,500 items to over 16 different charities in exactly ONE month!! UNBELIEVABLE!!"

The momentum never stopped. What began as one woman's birthday project grew into a movement of kindness that spread across neighborhoods, schools, and states. People began asking themselves: what's my fifty? Could I write fifty thank-you notes, bake for fifty minutes for a neighbor, donate fifty books, or give fifty dollars to a cause I love?

By the end of that first year, Kristen had supported far more than twelve charities. And three years later, What's Your 50? had blossomed into more than three hundred twenty-five projects across nine states.

Kristen didn't just mark a milestone birthday; she created a movement. One that shows how kindness multiplies when people are given a simple, joyful way to give. And it all began with one woman, who had a heart big enough to ask: What's Your 50?

(MKRO Kindness Award Winner, Nov 2021)

Reflection: Kristen reminds us that we can all give in small, joyful ways. What is one small way that you can help, perhaps in an easy and fun increment of 50?

People often ask me what the most effective technique is for transforming their lives. It is a little embarrassing that after years and years of research and experimentation. I have to say that the best answer is just be a little kinder.

– Aldous Huxley

TAKING OWNERSHIP

When a brutal summer heatwave swept through Portland, the air was heavy and unrelenting. Inside a small home on the east side, seventy-two-year-old J.C. Wade sat in the only room he and his two dogs could bear. The temperature outside had soared to dangerous levels, and inside wasn't much better. His small, fixed income didn't leave room for luxuries like air conditioning so J.C. was doing what he could, armed with a fan that mostly just moved hot air from one corner to another.

Then came a knock at the door. Volunteers from Taking Ownership PDX stood on his porch, holding a brand-new air conditioner. They wheeled it in, installed it, and within the hour, cool air was spilling into the room. Wade sat back in his chair; his dogs sprawled gratefully on the floor beside him. His eyes watered as he said, "It was just a small air conditioner, and it's in one room, but it was enough for me and my dogs to make it."

Moments like this are the heartbeat of Taking Ownership PDX, the grassroots movement founded by Portland activist Randal Wyatt in 2020. What began as a bold idea, to provide free repairs for Black homeowners and small businesses, has grown into a lifeline for families who have lived through decades of displacement, redlining, and gentrification.

"I wanted to help Black homeowners age in place, generate wealth, and keep predatory investors away," Randal explained. "The idea was simple: revive Black-owned homes and businesses to strengthen the communities that are still here."

At first, it was just Randal reaching out to homeowners, offering free improvements, and convincing people that yes, this was real, and no, there wasn't a catch. He gathered names of volunteers, contractors, and neighbors willing to lend a hand. A few projects turned into a few more, and suddenly this "small idea" had a whole lot of momentum.

Today, Taking Ownership PDX has more than six hundred volunteers, with new ones joining every week. Together, they've restored over one hundred sixty homes, doing everything from pulling weeds and painting fences to repairing decks, replacing windows, and installing new roofs. Homeowners often pitch in alongside the volunteers, creating scenes filled with laughter, sweat, and shared purpose.

Priority is always given to those who need it most: seniors, single parents, and people surviving on incomes under $20,000 a year. Urgent safety issues, like leaks or electrical hazards, jump to the front of the line. Right now, more than three hundred fifty homeowners are waiting for help. Each name represents a story, a family holding on in neighborhoods where rising prices threaten to push them out.

Randal has also built partnerships with local companies that donate appliances, materials, and skilled labor. From big projects like roof repairs to smaller but no less vital jobs like replacing a broken fridge, these efforts restore more than just buildings; they restore dignity, safety, and hope.

But for Randal, this work is about more than fixing homes. It's about reimagining what it means to be a neighbor. "As neighborhoods get more affluent, the standard of upkeep changes," he said. "Instead of calling the city on your neighbor, why not walk over, ask what's going on, and offer to help?"

That mindset is spreading. Every repaired deck, every patched roof, every air conditioner handed to a grateful elder is a ripple of kindness that strengthens community bonds. Randal's vision is not just about keeping Black families in their homes; it's about nurturing a culture of care, empathy, and justice in a city that too often forgets its roots.

One air conditioner. One roof. One garden weeded. Each act may seem small, but together, they are rewriting the story of Portland's Black community. And at the center of it all is a simple question Randal poses every day, not just to himself, but to all of us:

What does it mean to truly take ownership of our communities?

(MKRO Kindness Grant Winner, Feb 2022)

> **Reflection:** Randal's dedication shows how grassroots efforts, empathy, and collaboration can protect generational wealth, fight injustice, and build stronger communities for everyone. What is one way you could bring kindness into your community?

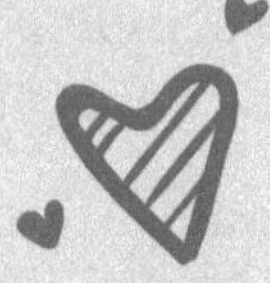

*Kindness has a beautiful way
of reaching down into a weary heart
and making it shine like
the rising sun.*

– Unknown

WHEN KINDNESS FIGHTS BACK

A freshman girl stood frozen in the bathroom stall, staring at her phone as the cruel messages kept flashing across the screen. The words cut deep harsh, mocking, and relentless. By the time she walked back into the hallway, the whispers and side glances made it clear: she was the joke of the day.

That girl was Valerianne Hinkley. At fourteen years old, she carried the weight of being singled out, bullied until she felt small, isolated, and completely invisible. For a while, she believed the lie the bullies wanted her to believe. But one day, after leaving school early and crying quietly in her room, something shifted.

"Enough is enough," she told herself. "If I'm feeling this way, I know others are, too. And I don't want anyone else to feel this alone."

That moment of heartbreak became the seed of something extraordinary. Instead of letting cruelty define her, Valerianne decided to fight back with kindness. She launched the Be Bold Stand Up to Bullying campaign and started small, with sticky notes. Brightly colored Post-its, each handwritten with encouragement: You are worth it. You are loved. You are awesome.

The next morning, she plastered her high school lockers with more than eight hundred of them. Imagine a student walking up to their locker, bracing for another hard day, only to find a note telling them they mattered. Smiles spread. Shoulders lifted. For the first time in a long while, kids felt seen.

That was just the beginning. What started as a hallway covered in encouragement turned into Valerianne's signature project, the Positive Post-it Note campaign. She brought the project to multiple schools and community events, inspiring other local schools to start their own versions. What began as a quiet act of encouragement turned into a full-on movement.

Through her experiences, Valerianne came to understand something important: you never really know what someone else is carrying. Not every student goes home to supportive parents or a safe environment. Sometimes the kids who bully are themselves hurting, repeating cycles of pain they've learned. To Valerianne, kindness and respect aren't just nice gestures; they're the first steps in breaking those cycles.

Her acts were simple, but their impact was profound. For someone feeling invisible, a Post-it note could be the difference between despair and hope.

But Valerianne didn't just want to spread kindness; she wanted to create lasting change. She stood in front of her school board and bravely shared her own story, pushing for stronger protections against bullying. Her voice helped reshape the district's Student Code of Conduct, adding clear language on bullying and harassment. She studied Maine's anti-bullying laws and worked with the state's Department of Education, determined to make the system stronger for the next student who might feel what she once felt.

The numbers tell a hard truth: one in five U.S. students between the age of twelve and eighteen report being bullied each year. More than 160,000 teens skip school every day out of fear. Valerianne's mission is to change those numbers, not just with policies, but with compassion.

Her Be Bold Stand Up to Bullying campaign continues to remind students that they are not alone, that their worth is not up for debate, and that kindness can change the course of a day, or even a life.

Valerianne once stood in a hallway, believing she didn't belong. Today, because of her courage, countless others know that they do.

(MKRO Kindness Award Winner, May 2022)

> **Reflection:** Valerianne's courage to confront bullying turned her pain into powerful advocacy, reminding us that kindness and standing up for others can create safer, more compassionate communities. What would our schools, workplaces, and communities look like if kindness were the guiding principle?

We are meant to live in joy. This does not mean that life will be easy or painless. It means that we can turn our faces to the wind and accept that this is the storm we must pass through. We cannot succeed by denying what exists. The acceptance of reality is the only place from which change can begin.

– Desmond Tutu

HOPE TAKES THE FIELD

A boy no older than eight stood barefoot on a dusty patch of ground in a refugee camp in Greece. His shirt was torn, his eyes dull, his shoulders heavy with the weight of things no kid should have to carry. When Stephen Schirra placed a brand-new soccer ball in his hands, the boy hesitated at first, as if the gift couldn't possibly be meant for him. He stared at it, then at Stephen, then back at the ball. And then it happened. A smile spread across his face, wide, unguarded, pure joy.

Within seconds, other kids rushed over, and soon that dusty patch of ground turned into a full-on soccer field. Laughter, shouting, wild kicks in every direction. For a few beautiful minutes, the trauma of war took a backseat. For a moment, they were just kids playing a game.

Stephen never forgot that boy, or the way something as simple as a soccer ball could unlock hope where hope felt impossible. It's why he founded Around the Worlds, a non-profit dedicated to bringing soccer, joy, and healing to children living in some of the world's most vulnerable communities.

"I grew up playing soccer, like most kids in the U.S.," Stephen says. "I never thought twice about having access to fields, uniforms, and coaches. It was just normal. But when you see children who have lost everything light up because of a ball, it changes you. It makes you want to do more."

From refugee camps to orphanages, from shelters for trafficked children to schools in war-torn countries, Stephen has traveled the globe teaching free soccer workshops. Each session ends with the gift of soccer balls and gear, so the game and the joy don't end when he leaves. "The ball is more than a toy," Stephen explains. "It's a tool. It teaches teamwork, resilience, and belief in yourself. And for many of these kids, it's the first time anyone has handed them something brand-new, something just for them."

Stephen's journey to this calling started long before he boarded planes to Pakistan, Rwanda, or Nicaragua. Growing up in Ellington, Connecticut, he was the kid who stayed late after practice to help clean up, who volunteered as a coach, who worked with the Special Olympics, who spent weekends mentoring youth in inner-city programs. "Giving back always felt natural," he says. "But over time, that local passion became a global calling."

Now, wherever he goes, Stephen sees soccer breaking barriers between children divided by war, between cultures separated by fear, between kids who believed their futures had been stolen. "The game has this unmatched ability to transcend boundaries," he says. "Race, religion, gender, language, it doesn't matter. On the field, everyone belongs."

The impact is staggering. So far, Around the Worlds has reached children in sixty-nine countries, donated over five thousand soccer balls, and created moments of joy for nearly ten thousand kids. But numbers don't capture the full story. The real measure is in the boy who kicked a ball for the first time and laughed until he fell over. The girl who learned she could lead a team and realized she could lead in life. The children who once carried only fear and now carry dreams.

For Stephen, every workshop is a reminder of why he started. "I want these kids to know they matter. That their lives have value. That even in the darkest places, joy is possible."

Through his compassion and vision, Stephen is showing the world that soccer is far more than a game. It's a lifeline, a bridge to healing, and a spark that can reignite hope in children who need it most.

(MKRO Kindness Grant Winner, Aug 2022)

> **Reflection:** Stephen's story shows us how a simple game like soccer can become a powerful tool for healing, empowerment, and hope. What small act of kindness has stayed with you long after it happened?

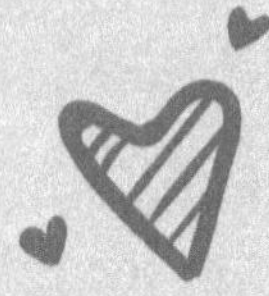

Kindness takes us beyond our own thoughts and feelings to the concerns of others, which enlarges our perspective. A bigger view makes our daily ups and downs look smaller. Kindness allows us to be grateful.

– Sakyong Mipham

THE KINDNESS AMBASSADOR

At just nine years old, Silas Scauzillo showed the world that kindness has no age limit. While most kids were busy with sports or video games, Silas was busy changing lives. Now fifteen years old, he continues to inspire, but it's those early years of heart-led leadership earned him the MKRO Kindness Award.

Silas's journey began with someone very close to his heart: his baby sister, Gianna, who was born with Down Syndrome. Watching the way some people overlooked her or failed to see her worth lit a spark in Silas. He decided no one should ever feel left out or invisible. At just seven years old, he rallied friends together to form the Kindness Squad. Their mission was simple: sprinkle kindness and pay it forward. No capes required.

They started small: helping a classmate pick up dropped books, inviting the shy kid to sit at lunch, making cards for neighbors. But here's the thing about kindness, it spreads. Before long, families in other communities, even in other states, were joining in. Turns out a group of kids being kind is more powerful than we give it credit for.

Silas didn't stop there. He began saving his allowance to buy little gifts: stickers, bubbles, toy cars, and notebooks from local shops. He'd leave them in parks and playgrounds with a "Random Act of Kindness" card attached, inviting whoever found the gift to pass it along. Parents later shared stories of their children finding these surprises and grinning from ear to ear. Strangers found themselves reminded, in the middle of an ordinary day, that kindness is alive and well.

But perhaps Silas's most moving vision was his dream of Buddy Benches, special benches placed in schoolyards where kids who felt lonely could sit, signaling they needed a friend. To Silas, these benches weren't just a place to rest. They were an invitation. They said, "You matter. You belong. Someone will come sit with you." He imagined schools where compassion was part of the culture, where kids automatically reached out to each other.

Teachers began calling him a "kindness ambassador." Friends said he made it impossible to feel invisible, because Silas always noticed the person on the edge of the crowd. Whether it was offering a smile, sharing a seat, or simply saying, "Hey, want to play?" he had a way of dissolving walls.

His neighbors still remember the little boy with the big heart who insisted that kindness wasn't something you did occasionally, it was who you were. He showed that holding a door open or speaking up for someone being teased wasn't small at all. It was world changing.

Today, Silas continues to lead with empathy, still carrying forward the lessons his sister first taught him. His vision hasn't changed: he wants a world where acceptance is the norm, not the exception, and where kindness isn't random, but expected.

Silas's story is a reminder that you're never too young, or too small, to make a big difference. His ripple of kindness, sparked by love for his sister, has already touched countless lives, and it continues to grow, one small act at a time.

(MKRO Kindness Award Winner, May 2019)

> **Reflection:** Silas reminds us that kindness is strongest when we look out for one another. What does kindness mean to you in your everyday life? How can you embody that meaning in your interactions with others?

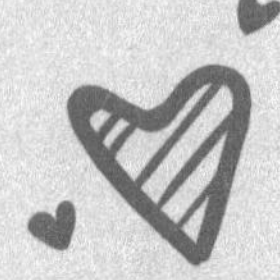

The heart is always the place to go.

– Ayya Khema

A LIFE OF KINDNESS

On a December evening not long ago, a grandmother in Berlin, Maryland, sat at her kitchen table staring at a stack of unpaid bills. Her heart ached as she thought about her two young grandchildren asleep in the next room. Their parents were no longer in the picture, and suddenly the responsibility of raising them had fallen to her. She worried about rent, food, and whether she could afford even a single Christmas gift.

And then, a letter arrived.

One envelope stood out. It was addressed to her grandson, written in bright, looping handwriting. Inside, on thick, festive paper, was a message from Santa Claus himself. And not a generic "ho ho ho" situation either, this Santa knew things. He told the little boy how proud he was of him, how kind he'd been, how loved and special he was. As the boy read it out loud, his eyes grew wider by the sentence. By the end, he was beaming like he'd just been personally invited to the North Pole.

His grandmother? Full-on tears. The good kind. The kind that loosen the knot in your chest. For the first time in weeks, the weight lifted just a bit. Someone, somewhere, cared enough to make her grandson feel seen.

That someone was Colby Phillips.

Every Christmas, Colby writes and mails thousands of personalized letters from Santa, sometimes to children, sometimes to adults who could use a spark of joy. It's just one of countless acts of kindness she quietly makes part of her life, but it captures who she is: a woman who notices when others are struggling and finds a way, however big or small, to ease their burden.

Colby's story is woven into her community through moments like these. Ask around Berlin, and you'll hear story after story. Like the time she organized a Christmas celebration for a young man battling stage 4 cancer, determined to bring light into his darkest days. They'll recall how she launched a support group after losing a friend to suicide, creating a safe space for people struggling with depression. They'll tell you about the fires, the floods, the countless personal tragedies where Colby simply showed up, often before anyone else thought to.

Her generosity isn't reserved for organized events; it's instinctual. Years ago, while working at a waterfront restaurant, Colby heard a security guard shouting that children were in danger in the water. She was still wearing her tuxedo shirt and bow tie when she ran toward the noise, and then promptly dove into the frigid, raging Atlantic Ocean that November day. No pause, no overthinking. She helped rescue nine people that day. She hadn't stopped to calculate the risk or wait for someone else to act. She just moved. Because that's what Colby does.

Over the years, her acts of kindness have rippled outward, feeding hungry families, clothing children, lifting up grieving neighbors, and encouraging strangers through her daily uplifting blog posts. She doesn't do it for recognition; in fact, most of her work goes unheralded until someone she's helped nominates her for an award. Colby was nominated for the MKRO Kindness Award three separate times, an almost unheard-of distinction that reflects just how deeply she touches the lives around her.

Colby doesn't treat kindness as an occasional gesture. For her, it's a way of life, a daily decision to show up, reach out, and remind others they are not alone. She has proven, time and again, that one person's compassion can ripple across an entire community.

For the grandmother at her kitchen table, that ripple looked like a letter from Santa that restored a little boy's belief in magic and gave her hope when she needed it most.

(MKRO Kindness Award Winner, Nov 2022)

Reflection: Colby's life is a powerful example of living kindness as a daily practice. How could you make kindness a habit, not just an occasional act?

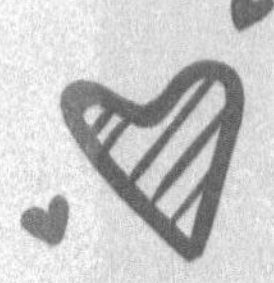

*What sunshine is to flowers, smiles
are to humanity.*

– Joseph Addison

KINDNESS, LIVED DAILY

<hr>

Adam Rosante doesn't just talk about kindness; he casually lives it. His life is a steady, quiet masterclass in showing up for people, and his generosity has touched people in ways he may never fully realize.

We first learned about Adam through a simple Facebook post that stopped us in our tracks. Alongside a photo of Keith Flint, the late lead singer of Prodigy, Adam wrote about how Flint's death by suicide nearly five years ago had inspired him to do something small but extraordinary. He decided that every Tuesday, he would keep his schedule open for anyone who needed to talk. No script, no advice, no judgment, just a listening ear.

"It's not therapy," Adam explained. "It's not a replacement for that. It's simply a free and friendly ear."

At first, people were hesitant. Strangers would message him and say, "I don't really know why I'm calling, but I saw your post and felt like I should reach out." And yet, week after week, those conversations unfolded. Some were heavy, some tentative, others filled with long pauses. But all of them had one thing in common: they left people lighter than when they came.

Think about the courage it takes for someone sitting alone in their room, weighed down by the thought that they have no one to turn to, to pick up the phone and call a stranger. And think about the kindness of the man on the other end, Adam, who chooses, over and over again, to simply listen. That is humanity at its most raw and most beautiful.

But Adam's kindness didn't stop there. His life became a mission to find where the world was hurting and step in with love.

In 2017, he visited an urban farm in Harlem and learned that many children there, just blocks away from some of the wealthiest parts of Manhattan, were going hungry every single weekend. During the week, they had access to subsidized meals at school. But on Saturdays and Sundays, their fridges were empty. The thought of kids going to bed hungry just a subway ride from Wall Street shook Adam to his core. He spoke with the school principal and promised to do something.

That promise became Good Eats, a nonprofit that quietly transforms weekends for children in need. Every Friday, volunteers pack unmarked backpacks with healthy food, breakfast, lunch, dinner, and snacks, and place them in the hands of children who otherwise might not eat until Monday. On Monday morning, the backpacks are returned, ready to be filled again.

It's a simple system, but in its simplicity lies dignity, care, and life-changing impact. What started in Harlem has since expanded to Los Angeles, with Adam's team nourishing hundreds of children every week.

When asked about it, Adam said, "We're a lean organization. Every dollar goes into the bellies of hungry children. None of us takes a paycheck. This work is our honor and privilege."

And yet, Adam decided he could still do more. In 2023, he founded HomeKeeper, a nonprofit with a mission as intimate as it is vital: helping single moms and their children stay in their homes. These are families doing everything right, yet living so close to the edge that one surprise expense, one unexpected car repair, medical bill, or missed shift could mean eviction. Worse still, many don't qualify for assistance.

So HomeKeeper steps in at the scariest moment. When a family is on the brink of losing their home, Adam and his team step in and cover at least one month of their rent or mortgage. That gift of breathing room allows families to regroup, catch up, and, perhaps for the first time, start building a small savings account.

Imagine the relief of a mom who's been lying awake at night, wondering how to keep a roof over her children's heads, terrified of what comes next, suddenly realizing she won't have to pack them into a shelter or a car. That is the gift Adam gives. And he does it quietly, without fanfare, because for him, kindness isn't about recognition. It's about relief.

In a time when the world often feels divided and harsh, Adam's unwavering kindness is a reminder that love, generosity, and presence are still among the most powerful forces we have. He is not just a kindness hero; he is living proof of the change one person can make when they choose, day after day, to show up for others.

(MKRO Kindness Award Winner, Apr 2025)

> **Reflections:** Adam shows us that kindness is about being present for others in whatever way they need, whether it's a listening ear, food on the table, or a helping hand to keep a home. Pay attention this week to the moments when kindness shows up around you. How do those moments impact you? How can you create more of them?

Since I'm not sure of the address to which to send my gratitude, I put it out there in everything I do.

– Michael J. Fox

BRIDGING BORDERS WITH COMPASSION

The woman sat across from Taha, clutching her jaw, her eyes wet with pain. She had been living in the United States for months but still hadn't seen a dentist. The infection that began in her tooth had spread, leaving her weak and feverish. It wasn't because she didn't want care, she simply didn't know how to ask for it. She didn't have the language, didn't understand the system, and didn't know where to turn. So she sat there, hurting and hoping.

For Taha Umar, that moment hit hard. Because he knew she wasn't an exception, she was the rule. Behind her were countless refugee families who had fled war or persecution only to find themselves battling new, quieter struggles in a country that promised safety. Illnesses went untreated, appointments were missed, and health problems grew worse, not because they lacked courage, but because access is complicated, confusing, and honestly kind of overwhelming even for people who've lived here forever.

Taha understood this in his bones. As the son of two immigrant parents and an immigrant himself, he watched his own family navigate new systems, new expectations, and a new language. The healthcare barrier alone can feel like trying to read a foreign manual while already exhausted. But unlike many refugees, his family had a community to lean on. Others weren't so lucky.

So Taha showed up where he could. He volunteered at a local refugee resettlement agency, sorting donations, setting up apartments, and eventually leading an English Language Learning Lab. He taught everyday survival English, banking, transportation, filling out forms, clicking the right buttons online. He saw how much dignity returned to people when they gained the tools to communicate. And that's where something clicked.

He watched highly educated doctors, teachers, and engineers, people who had once been leaders in their fields, feel completely powerless trying to navigate a grocery store or medical check-in. And when they finally found their voices? The shift was instant. Confidence returned. Dignity came back online. It changed them. And it changed him.

But the stories of untreated illness never left him. Teaching language was powerful, but it wasn't enough. People were still getting sick. Still going without care. Still hurting in silence.

So, in August 2022, at just nineteen years old, Taha founded Refugee Health Connection (RHC), a student-led nonprofit with a simple but powerful mission: to tear down the barriers keeping refugees from healthcare. RHC runs workshops that explain how the U.S. healthcare system actually works, from making an appointment, to knowing what questions to ask, to understanding what insurance even means. The goal isn't just treatment, it's empowerment.

He also launched the Care Kit Assembly Initiative, providing refugee families with basic essentials many of us don't think twice about: toothbrushes, toothpaste, floss, bandages, wipes, and more. For families starting over with nothing, these kits are often the first moment they feel prepared instead of panicked.

What began with Taha's heartbreak at a single woman's suffering has grown into a movement. Today, Refugee Health Connection includes 30 student volunteers and an advisory board with medical professionals, ensuring every resource is clear, accurate, and compassionate.

When asked why he does this, Taha points back to his roots. "Thankfully, my parents overcame their challenges by forming bonds with other immigrants who helped them along the way," he says. "I want to be that person for others."

With refugees continuing to arrive from Afghanistan, Ukraine, and beyond, Taha knows the work is only beginning. "I'm a firm believer in health equity," he says. "Everyone deserves an equal opportunity to be as healthy as they can be."

One teenager saw a problem most people walk right past, and instead of looking away, he rolled up his sleeves. In doing so, Taha is not just changing healthcare access; he's restoring dignity, hope, and the simple, profound belief that every life is worth caring for.

(MKRO Kindness Grant Winner, Feb 2023)

Reflection: Taha's story reminds us that empathy combined with education and action can break down barriers and restore dignity. If you could deliver a message of hope to someone who's struggling, what would you say? Write it down and share it with someone who needs to hear it.

*Nothing can make our lives,
or the lives of other people,
more beautiful than
perpetual kindness.*

– Leo Tolstoy

A BUNDLE OF COMPASSION

When Rachael Rosenberg offered a care bundle to a woman sitting on the sidewalk outside a Los Angeles convenience store, she didn't expect much more than a polite nod. Instead, the woman hugged the socks in the bundle to her chest, her expression transforming into pure, overwhelming gratitude. Tears welled up in her eyes; she hadn't owned a clean pair in months. In that moment, the look on her face said it all: after being overlooked by so many, the simple act of being seen and cared for moved her beyond words.

That moment stayed with Rachael. She was only thirteen at the time, preparing for her bat mitzvah, but she understood something profound: being homeless wasn't just about lacking shelter or food, it was about being unseen. And she knew she couldn't walk away from that truth.

Rachael wasn't new to helping. She had already spent time volunteering through her synagogue, making sandwiches and packing meals with her family. But the more she listened to unhoused people talk about what they actually needed, the clearer it became: a sandwich is great, but it's not the whole story. People needed socks (apparently the real gold standard), blankets, first aid supplies, hygiene items, sunscreen and sometimes even food for their pets. They needed care that was both practical and personal.

So, in December 2018, she launched Bundles of Kindness, with a bold goal to assemble one hundred survival kits. And these weren't thrown-together bags. Each bundle was thoughtfully packed with a sleeping mat, a blanket, fresh socks and underwear, toiletries, menstrual products, sunscreen, shelf-stable food, water, juice, first aid items, and a flyer with community resources. She even added extras often overlooked, flip-flops, jackets, and pet supplies, because, as one man once told her, "When you're living on the street, even little things keep you going."

Pretty soon, her family garage looked less like a garage and more like an organized kindness warehouse. Thanks to her outreach and a growing Amazon Wish List, donations poured in. In June 2019, she gathered volunteers at her synagogue to help assemble the bundles, turning piles of supplies into care packages brimming with dignity. But for Rachael, the most important part was always the delivery, hand-to-hand, face-to-face.

"Bundles of Kindness' mission is to provide basic necessities while offering human interaction, dignity, love, and kindness," Rachael explained. For her, the supplies were only half the story. What mattered just as much was looking someone in the eye, listening to their story, and showing them that they mattered.

One recipient put it simply: "Just having someone see me, smile at me, and tell me I can survive this, that meant more than the food."

Since then, Rachael has distributed more than two thousand bundles. She now works out of a storage unit instead of her family's garage, delivering kits to food pantries, mobile showers, shelters, safe parking programs, teen drop-in centers, and directly into the hands of people she meets on the street. She even keeps a few bundles in her car, ready at a moment's notice.

Her work is not just charity, it's a transformation. Through Bundles of Kindness, Rachael is changing lives, one heartfelt interaction at a time. Her leadership shows that compassion doesn't wait for adulthood. It begins the moment we decide to notice, to care, and to act.

(MKRO Kindness Grant Winner, Mar 2023)

Reflection: Rachael's journey epitomizes how youthful passion combined with thoughtful action can provide not just essential needs but also dignity and empathy to those often overlooked. Who inspires you with their kindness? Write them a note to let them know the impact they've made in your life. Or better yet, nominate them for the Matt Kurtz Kindness Award.

Realize that for every ongoing war and religious outrage and environmental devastation, there are a thousand counter-balancing acts of staggering generosity and humanity and art and beauty happening all over the world, right now, on a breathtaking scale, from flower box to cathedral.

– Mark Morford

SIDEWALKS OF HOPE

One gray winter morning in Cheboygan, Michigan, Susan Melton bent down on the icy pavement, her fingers stiff from the cold as she scribbled three words in bright pink chalk: You are enough. A man walking his dog slowed to watch. He paused, reading the words once, then again. His eyes welled up. "I needed that today," he whispered, almost to himself, before walking on.

Moments like that are why Susan keeps going. For more than twelve years, she has been chalking one message every single day, words of encouragement, hope, and resilience, for anyone who might happen to pass by. Rain, wind, or snow doesn't stop her. If the sidewalks are buried in snow, she scrapes them clear before chalking quickly, her breath hanging in the air like smoke. What began as a small summer project in 2011 has grown into a daily ritual of kindness that has touched lives far beyond her small Michigan town.

The idea didn't come from lightness but from struggle. Susan was wrestling with depression, searching desperately for something to pull herself out of the darkness. At first, she tried writing affirmations on sticky notes and plastering them around her home, tiny reminders to keep going. But the words felt too contained, too private. They helped her, but she wondered: what if they could help someone else too?

That thought took root after she watched the film What the Bleep Do We Know!?, which included a segment about how even plants respond to positive or negative words. If plants could be changed by affirmations, what about people? Susan picked up a box of sidewalk chalk and set herself a simple challenge: write at least one positive message in public every day.

"I thought, maybe if I put this out there where other people can see it, it will make them feel better," she recalls. "And maybe it will make me feel better too."

Three months passed. Then six. Then fall came, and Susan realized she couldn't stop. The chalk messages had become her lifeline, a way of grounding herself, and they were becoming lifelines for strangers, too. People started stopping her on the street, thanking her, even confessing that her words had reached them on days they were quietly struggling.

Now, fifteen years later, Susan hasn't missed a single day. Not one. She carries chalk everywhere she goes, leaving messages not only in Cheboygan but also in other cities and states when she travels. "I chalk fast," she laughs, "but I never skip."

Eventually, she began snapping photos of her messages and sharing them online. The response was overwhelming. A simple Facebook page turned into a community where people around the world began following along, and some even started their own chalk projects inspired by her. From sidewalks in Michigan to paths in other countries, her words now ripple far beyond the places she's ever stood.

Susan knows it might look like a small gesture, words that will wash away in the next rain. But to her, the impermanence is part of the beauty. The words are there when someone needs them most.

"It's a tiny thing," she says softly, "but if I know I'm helping even one person, that makes all the difference in the world."

Susan's chalk is simple, but her message is timeless: kindness doesn't have to be big to be powerful. Sometimes it's just a few bright words on a gray sidewalk that remind someone, in the moment they need it most, that they matter.

(MKRO Kindness Award Winner, May 2023)

Reflection: What small act could you repeat daily, like Susan with her chalk, to create ripples in your own community? Write it down and try to make it happen this week.

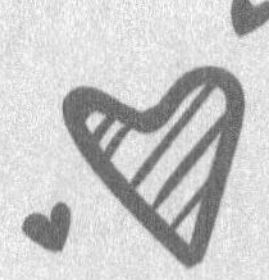

I swear I will not dishonor my soul with hatred, but offer myself humbly as a guardian of nature, as a healer of misery, as a messenger of wonder, as an architect of peace.

– Diane Ackerman

SHELTERING WITH COMPASSION

The wind was sharp that January night, the kind that slices through even the thickest coat. On the boardwalk in Ocean City, Maryland, most storefronts were dark, their summer crowds long gone. But at the Cold Weather Shelter, the doors swung open, and Jason and Trisha Long stood ready to greet each person who shuffled in from the cold. Not with fanfare or speeches, just with open arms. One man shuffled in, hands trembling, clutched a blanket that had clearly seen better days. Trisha smiled warmly, gently took the blanket from him, and handed him clean sheets, a towel, and pointed him toward a hot meal waiting nearby. The man's shoulders eased. "Thank you," he whispered, as if the words weren't nearly enough.

Moments like this are why Jason and Trisha keep showing up, winter after winter. Since 2015, they have dedicated themselves to caring for Ocean City's homeless population during the coldest and most dangerous months of the year. From

November through March, when temperatures plunge and the resort town's bustle gives way to silence, they make sure the shelter is open, staffed, and stocked with everything needed to keep people safe and warm.

It's not glamorous work. It means coordinating meals, gathering supplies, and finding volunteers to cover the long overnight shifts. And when no one else can do it, Jason and Trisha fill in themselves, sacrificing sleep and comfort to make sure no one must face the night outside.

What makes their work extraordinary is not just the logistics, it's the way they treat each guest. As volunteer, Patti Stevens, wrote: "What inspires me most is the respect and care they show. They don't just give someone a bed. They bring in stylists for haircuts, help people get IDs or Social Security documents, and even find urgent health and dental care. They see each guest as a person with dignity, not a statistic."

Inside the shelter, guests are welcomed like family. There's a hot dinner and real conversation around the table. Showers and laundry are available, and in the morning, coffee and pastries are ready before everyone heads back out. Volunteers register each guest, share stories, and sometimes simply sit with someone who needs to feel seen.

"Freezing to death is preventable," one volunteer said. "We don't want people dying outside just because they're homeless."

Jason is quick to point out that while donations are vital, volunteers are the true lifeblood of the shelter. "Monetary donations can get us the stuff," he explains, "but volunteers are number one." He and Trisha serve on the shelter's board alongside others who share the same commitment, and together they've built a network of compassion that keeps the doors open.

The COVID-19 pandemic made everything harder. Guidelines shifted daily, risks multiplied, and isolation deepened. But Jason and Trisha didn't waver. They worked tirelessly to adapt, ensuring the shelter could stay open safely at a time when the need was greater than ever.

Trisha is keenly aware of the misconceptions that swirl around homelessness. "There's a preconceived notion that homeless people are dangerous or difficult," she says. "But that's not the case. When they get here, they're so thankful. We're often the only warm place and hot meal they have."

In a town known for beach vacations and summer fun, Jason and Trisha have made winter a season of survival and grace. Their kindness reaches people in the rawest, most vulnerable moments of their lives. For those who walk through the shelter doors, it's not just a bed or a meal, it's proof that someone cares enough to stand in the cold with them until the morning comes.

(MKRO Kindness Award Winner, Jun 2023)

> **Reflections:** Jason and Trisha show how compassion and community can provide not only warmth but also dignity and hope to those in need. How can you celebrate and encourage kindness in your family? Brainstorm one idea and put it into action.

Doing nothing for others is the undoing of ourselves. We must be purposely kind and generous, or we miss the best part of existence.

– Horace Mann

TURNING PAGES, CHANGING LIVES

In Larry Abrams' twelfth-grade classroom in Lindenwold, NJ, a quiet moment changed everything. He was chatting with one of his students when she mentioned, almost off-handedly, that she never read to her two-year-old child. Larry paused, stunned. "Not even bedtime stories?" he asked gently, trying not to sound as alarmed as he felt. She shook her head. There were no books in her home, and then she added, very matter-of-factly, "Reading is not part of my culture."

That moment broke something open in Larry. Here was a bright young woman, already juggling school and motherhood, but her baby was growing up in a home without books. No bedtime stories. No favorite characters. No pages being turned by chubby little hands. He couldn't stop thinking about it. If this toddler has no books, how many others were growing up the same way?

Larry had already seen the consequences. He saw it every day. Many of his ninth graders struggled to read at even a fifth-grade level. And he knew the truth we don't like to say out loud: when kids miss that early window, the gap doesn't stay small. It grows. Reading isn't just about school; it's about confidence, communication, and believing you belong in the world.

Determined to act, Larry went home that night and posted a simple request to friends and family: "If you have any gently used children's books, I'll make sure they get into the hands of families who need them." He expected a handful of donations. Instead, his garage filled with over one thousand books.

Larry loaded them into boxes and brought them to young mothers and elementary schools in his community. He watched the way children's faces lit up as they cradled their very first books, holding them like treasures. Some pressed the covers to their chests. Others flipped pages eagerly, as if afraid someone might take them back. In that moment, Larry realized this was bigger than a single project; it was a mission.

He soon discovered he was teaching in what's called a "book desert." In these areas, families are stretched thin just trying to cover rent, food, and diapers. Books, however valuable, simply don't make the cut. "Some families are a paycheck away from disaster," Larry explained. "Books are often seen as a luxury. That's where we come in."

In 2017, Larry founded BookSmiles with a simple but radical belief: every child deserves to grow up surrounded by books. He set a goal that no child in his community would start kindergarten without a personal library at home.

Today, BookSmiles has given away nearly four million books. Through school partnerships, book drives, and even food banks, families now leave with groceries and stories. Dinner and bedtime reading? That's a win-win.

And every book represents more than just paper and ink. It's a parent and child curled up together at bedtime. It's a kid discovering the magic of words. It's a teenager finding their voice in literature.

Larry says it best, "Giving kids books almost ensures academic success. And every child in America should have that chance. Language is power."

Thanks to BookSmiles, thousands of children who once faced a future without stories now grow up in homes where words flow freely, where imaginations spark, and where stories whisper possibility.

All because Larry noticed what was missing and decided to do something about it. And sometimes, that's all it takes to change a child's story, one book at a time.

(MKRO Kindness Grant Winner, Aug 2023)

> **Reflections:** Larry shows us that giving kids access to books is more than charity; it's planting seeds for their future, helping them imagine, learn, and grow. How do you hope your acts of kindness will ripple out into the world?

However gloomy your situation, the world abounds in beauty, should you choose to see it.

– Jennifer Reese

THE POWER OF
SMALL WISHES

Ruby Chitsey was just eleven years old when a quiet moment in a nursing home changed her life forever.

She had accompanied her mom, a nurse practitioner, on a visit and found herself standing near the glass front doors as a resident's dog was being led away. Ruby noticed the woman's eyes following the dog, her expression shadowed with sadness. Curious, Ruby gently asked what was wrong.

The woman looked at her and said, "That's my dog . . . I don't know when I'll see her again."

Ruby learned the reason wasn't complicated or dramatic. The woman simply couldn't afford the $40 monthly fee to keep her dog with her. Forty dollars. That was it. And in that moment, Ruby had a realization that many adults never quite get to: if something so small could cause that much sadness, what other "little things" were quietly out of reach for people living there?

So Ruby started asking residents a simple question: "If you could have any three things in the world, what would they be?"

Ruby was stunned. No talk of riches, no dream vacations. The answers were never extravagant. One woman said she wanted some fresh fruit, a pair of pants that fit, and cat food for her beloved pet. Another wished for a soft blanket, a Diet Coke, or shampoo that smelled like home. These weren't grand dreams. They were quiet needs, tiny luxuries that offered comfort, dignity, and the feeling of being seen.

That moment cracked Ruby's heart wide open. "I realized the things they wanted were so small," she said later. "And if I could make them happen, then why wouldn't I?"

And just like that, Three Wishes for Ruby's Residents was born.

It started with Ruby spending her allowance to buy small gifts and asking friends to help, and showing up with bags of simple gifts. Today, it's a nonprofit that has granted more than 40,000 wishes to seniors in long-term care facilities across the country.

The wishes are still simple, but their impact is profound: a soft blanket to replace scratchy sheets, a favorite brand of shampoo, new shoes, even something as small as a Diet Coke. Each gift is more than an object; it's recognition and love in a place where loneliness is often overwhelming.

Ruby is quick to point out why this work matters so much. "Over 90% of them see fewer than one visitor a month," she explains. "They're forgotten. But when we show up, when we listen, we remind them that they still matter."

The truth is most nursing home residents live on less than $40 a month for all personal needs beyond food and housing. That's supposed to cover toiletries, snacks, haircuts, and any extras that might bring joy or comfort. It's not nearly enough, which is why even something as ordinary as cat food or a fresh haircut can feel out of reach.

Ruby believes those small comforts aren't luxuries at all. They're the things that restore dignity, spark joy, and remind people they are loved. "Kindness is my hobby," she likes to say, but that's a wild understatement. what she's created is far more than a hobby. She's built a movement.

She now leads a "Kid Board," a group of young people helping her spread compassion, proving that kindness isn't bound by age. Together, they're teaching the world a simple truth: sometimes the most powerful way to change a life is through the smallest of gestures.

Every blanket delivered, every wish granted, every visit made is a reminder that we all deserve to be seen. And because one 11-year-old girl chose to listen, tens of thousands of seniors across the country now feel a little less alone.

Ruby's story shows us that kindness doesn't have to be grand to be life changing. Sometimes, it looks like grapes, a blanket, or a bag of cat food, and the courage of a child who decided to care.

(MKRO Kindness Grant Winner, Sept 2023)

> **Reflection:** Ruby's story shows that dignity often lives in the smallest details of daily life. What simple act of kindness could you offer today that might make someone feel seen, valued, and remembered?

The secret to leaving someone with a lasting impression is kindness.

– Unknown

WARM HANDS, WARM HEARTS

When a mom in Chicago tucked her young daughter's hands into a pair of store-bought gloves, her heart sank. The fingers didn't fit. They never did. Her daughter, born with Apert Syndrome, had webbed and fused fingers, and no matter how many pairs they tried, gloves from the store were always too tight, too uncomfortable, or simply impossible to wear.

On the surface, it sounds like a small thing. Gloves that don't fit, no big deal, right? Except it is a big deal when you're a kid and winter rolls around and once again the world reminds you it wasn't designed with you in mind. And for her mom, it was one more heartbreak in a long list of ways her daughter was left out.

So she did what we all do when we're upset, she called a friend. That friend was Rena Rosen.

Rena didn't have to imagine what if feels like to be different. Born with craniofacial differences herself, she had spent her life navigating a world that often didn't understand her. She knew the sting of being excluded, the weight of stares, the ache of wanting to belong. So, when her friend asked if she knew anyone who could help, Rena didn't hesitate.

She didn't know how to knit. She didn't even know where to begin. But she was determined. She put out a call, asked around and found someone willing to make a pair of custom gloves, stitched carefully, thoughtfully, and intentionally to fit one very special set of hands.

The day the gloves arrived, everything changed.

That little girl slipped them on and just... beamed. She flexed her fingers, held her hands out, and admired them like they were the coolest thing she'd ever owned. Because they were. For the first time, she had gloves made just for her. Not "close enough." Not "almost." But perfect.

That single act of kindness didn't just warm one pair of hands; it lit a spark.

From that first request, Knit for a Unique Fit was born. What began as one child's need has grown into a worldwide network of love. Through a Facebook group, Rena now connects knitters and crocheters with children and adults who have limb differences, matching uniquely made hands with lovingly crafted gloves.

Not long after, another family received a pair. This time it was a young boy, whose mother later shared, "He was over the moon, he wore them to sleep for two weeks straight. He just loves having real gloves. It was this blessing we didn't know we needed, but it made him feel so included with his brother and with other kids."

Over three hundred custom items have been lovingly made and sent to more than thirty countries. Parents request them. Adults who've lived their entire lives without properly fitting gloves request them. And knitters, beautiful, generous humans, step up again and again, donating their time, skill, and materials, because they know it's not just a glove they're making. It's belonging. It's dignity. It's joy.

Rena calls it "connecting uniquely made hands with uniquely crafted gloves." But really, it's about connection in the deepest sense, reminding people that they are seen, valued, and worthy of care, exactly as they are.

Her advice is simple, but powerful: "If you see someone who looks different, compliment them first and then enter into a conversation. It opens up dialogue. Kindness is the one thing that bonds us all together, and it's so easy. It makes a huge difference, and it settles everyone's nerves."

What started with one little girl's wish now stretches across the globe. Every stitch carries love. Every glove carries dignity. And thanks to Rena, countless people are learning that even the smallest acts of kindness can fit perfectly.

(MKRO Kindness Award Winner, Nov 2023)

> **Reflections:** Rena reminds us that kindness means noticing the little things that make people feel truly seen and included. Who in your life has experienced hardship recently? How could your kindness help them heal or feel supported?

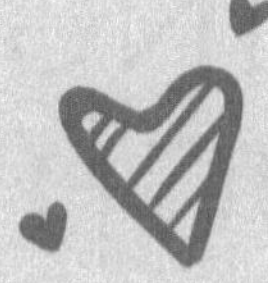

Worry less about what people think of you and simply get busy helping others in whatever way you can.

– Pope Francis

CHANGING MINDS THROUGH MUSIC

Ronald Braunstein stood on the conductor's podium, baton in hand, preparing to lead his orchestra through Beethoven's Fifth. To the audience, it looked like the usual scene: a seasoned maestro, elegant and confident, commanding the music with precision. What no one could see was the other performance happening inside him, a quiet tug-of-war of self-doubt, mood swings, and the constant weight of living with bipolar disorder.

For years, Ronald carried that struggle in silence, hiding it from colleagues and audiences alike, terrified that if anyone knew the truth, his career in classical music would crumble.

Then one day, the truth suddenly hit him. As he looked out at the faces in his orchestra, Ronald began to wonder how many of them were carrying hidden battles of their own. He had spent years believing he was alone in his struggle, but the more he paid attention, the more he sensed that others were quietly hurting, too, isolated by depression, anxiety, or illnesses they felt forced to hide. That realization cracked something open in him: if he wasn't alone, then perhaps he could be the one to build a place where no one else had to feel that way either.

That moment was the seed of Me2 Orchestra, the world's only classical music organization created specifically for people living with mental illness and the people who support them. It would be a place where no one had to apologize for panic attacks, medication side effects, or missed rehearsals due to therapy appointments. A place where music wasn't just about performance, but about survival, healing, and connection.

Ronald's path to that decision was remarkable. A Juilliard graduate, he had conducted orchestras around the world, from Europe, to Asia, to the United States. From the outside, it was all accolades and applause. Inside, it was a very different symphony. By the time he turned fifty-five, he realized his diagnosis wasn't something to be ashamed of; it was the reason he was uniquely positioned to create a new kind of orchestra, one that played not only for audiences, but for dignity, belonging, and hope.

Today, Me2 rehearsals feel different from any other orchestra. Musicians, some professionals, some amateurs, some living with schizophrenia, depression, bipolar disorder, or addiction, tune their instruments and settle into their seats. Ronald reminds them that here, the music matters, but the people matter more. If someone stumbles through a passage, the group waits patiently. If someone needs to step outside for a moment, no one whispers or judges. This isn't about perfection; it's about showing up as you are.

Their concerts reflect that same spirit. Audiences come expecting Brahms, Mozart, or Haydn, but what often lingers most are the personal stories woven between the music. A cellist might speak about how playing in Me2 is the only time she feels truly seen. A clarinetist might describe years of hiding his schizophrenia and the relief of finally belonging. After the last note fades, Ronald opens the floor for questions. The conversations that follow, raw, honest, and compassionate, chip away at the stigma that still surrounds mental illness.

What began as a small ensemble has grown into a movement. Me2 now includes more than two hundred musicians across multiple orchestras, chamber groups, and even a flute choir. Their model has spread internationally, inspiring affiliate programs that share the same mission: to create community through music, free from stigma.

The impact is profound. For many members, Me2 is more than an orchestra; it's a family. It's proof that they are not defined by their diagnosis, but by their humanity, their resilience, and the beauty they create together.

Ronald often says that kindness is built into every note they play. And he's right. In Me2, the music isn't just heard, it's felt deeply, by everyone in the room.

(MKRO Kindness Award Winner, Dec 2023)

Reflections: Ronald teaches us that embracing our challenges and expressing ourselves through creativity can break down stigma and bring people together in healing and hope. How might showing kindness to yourself help you show more kindness to others?

Help me to be less fearful of the measure of time, and more fully alive in the time that simply is. Help me to live time, not just to simply use it; to breathe it in, and return it in acts of love and presence.

– Avis Crowe

SERVING KINDNESS, ONE MEAL AT A TIME

When a young mother in San Diego, CA opened her front door in the spring of 2020, she wasn't expecting anyone. Her fridge was nearly empty, her kids were restless, and the weight of the pandemic had settled heavily on her shoulders. But there it was on her doorstep: a warm, steaming pan of lasagna, homemade, delivered by a stranger who simply wanted to help. She later admitted that she burst into tears, not because of the food itself, but because in that moment, she no longer felt invisible. Someone saw her. Someone cared.

That "someone" was Rhiannon Menn. A mom herself, Rhiannon knew what it felt like to be stretched thin. She listened as friends and neighbors confided their exhaustion, kids home from school, jobs shifting or disappearing, the isolation of uncertainty pressing down. "I wanted to do something," she remembers. "So, I figured, hey, I can cook a meal."

She didn't realize it then, but that small thought would grow into a movement that now spans the globe.

Rhiannon posted on Facebook, offering free lasagna dinners to anyone who needed one. And boom, requests poured in. She ordered ingredients in bulk from Costco, baked seven pans of lasagna, and drove across her community, leaving meals on doorsteps. With each delivery, she saw not just hunger being fed, but hearts being lifted.

Then something unexpected happened, others wanted in. Strangers began reaching out, asking if they could cook, too. Volunteers popped up from every corner, eager to share a little love from their own kitchens. The nonprofit Lasagna Love was born.

Today, those volunteers, affectionately called Lasagna Chefs, prepare and deliver meals to families they've never met. They pay for the ingredients themselves, but what they often talk about most isn't the food. It's the joy, purpose, and connection they feel while giving

The numbers are staggering. In just five years, Lasagna Love has fed 2.6 million people, powered by more than 80,000 volunteers worldwide. But the heart of the story is always in the tiny moments. Like the boy who wrapped his arms around his mother after a lasagna delivery, his face lit with relief as if to say, "we're not forgotten." Or the woman who admitted she had stopped believing in kindness until a warm meal showed up at her door.

"What we're really delivering," Rhiannon says, "is hope, connection, and the reminder that someone cares."

The ripple effect has been incredible. Many families who once received meals felt so moved that, when they were able, they signed up to cook for others. Kindness begets kindness, and what started as one mom's lasagna dish of comfort has become a worldwide chain of kindness.

Rhiannon dreams of the day her nonprofit will no longer be needed, not because the work isn't important, but because kindness itself will have returned to being second nature. "Our ultimate dream," she says, "is that neighborly kindness becomes everyday again."

One pan of lasagna. One family reached. One moment of kindness that has touched millions. Rhiannon's story reminds us that the simplest gestures can open doors not only to nourishment, but to belonging, and that a warm meal can sometimes be the first step toward healing a weary heart.

(MKRO Kindness Award Winner, Feb 2024)

> **Reflection:** Rhiannon's story shows how one small act of kindness can ignite a global movement. If every person you met today practiced one act of kindness, how would the world feel different?

*We can't heal the world today, but we
can begin with a voice of compassion,
a heart of love, an act of kindness.*

– Mary Davis

WHEELS OF JOY

The little boy's hands gripped the oversized button on the steering wheel, his eyes wide with nervous anticipation. For the first time, he wasn't watching from the sidelines as his siblings rode their bikes up and down the driveway; he was behind the wheel of his very own toy car. His mom crouched nearby, tears welling as she whispered encouragement: "Go ahead, sweetheart, you can do it." When the toy car lurched forward, his face broke into the kind of grin every parent remembers forever. For this child, living with a developmental disability that had made independent movement nearly impossible, that moment wasn't just play; it was freedom.

This is the magic that Aanand Mehta set out to create with Magical Motors, a nonprofit he co-founded to give children with developmental disabilities the chance to experience mobility, independence, and pure joy through adapted ride-on toy cars.

Aanand's journey began in 2019 while volunteering at the Neurologic Music Therapy Services of Arizona. There, he witnessed children working through therapies that demanded resilience and patience, and he saw up close the challenges they faced. He learned a staggering truth: 1 in 6 children in the U.S. lives with a developmental disability, yet access to pediatric mobility devices, like power wheelchairs, remains painfully limited. The cost alone, often several thousand dollars, puts these tools out of reach for many families.

Then Aanand's aha moment came from close to home. His cousin, Rohan Fichadia, had completed an Eagle Scout project building modified cars for kids with disabilities. What struck Aanand was how quickly and affordably Rohan could turn an ordinary toy car into something life changing. With just a few hours of work and some creative wiring, a child could go from being carried everywhere or left out, to driving their own car alongside their friends.

Together, Aanand and Rohan launched Magical Motors in 2021. Their mission was refreshingly simple: transform everyday toy cars into accessible vehicles that kids with developmental challenges could drive, cars that not only supported mobility but sparked joy.

Each car is carefully adapted. The pedals are rewired so that instead of relying on foot strength, the car can be powered by a large, easy-to-press button mounted on the steering wheel. Supportive seating, harnesses, and safety switches ensure kids are secure, giving parents peace of mind. Many cars come equipped with remote controls and stereos, because if you're going to drive, you might as well do it with style.

But the real magic isn't in the wiring. It's in the moments. Parents often describe the first drive as life changing. One mother shared how her son, who used to watch his brothers play from the porch, finally joined them in the driveway, beaming with pride. For families who have fought endless medical battles, this kind of moment feels like reclaiming a piece of childhood that disability too often steals.

Aanand didn't stop at building cars. Wanting to reach even more kids, he created a curriculum called Wheel Wizards, where high school students learn how to modify the cars themselves. In classrooms, students dive into wiring, design, and problem-solving, and then watch the joy their work creates when a child drives away in the very car they helped adapt.

In just a few years, Magical Motors has grown from a heartfelt idea into a movement of innovation and kindness. Each adapted car represents more than mobility; it's a symbol of possibility, independence, and belonging.

Aanand often says what they're really giving kids is not just a way to move, but a way to participate. A way to laugh alongside siblings, to chase a ball, to feel the thrill of control and freedom. And for parents, it's a powerful reminder that their child is not defined by limitations, but by potential.

Through creativity and compassion, Aanand is proving that even small engines can drive big change. Magical Motors isn't just about cars; it's about rewriting what childhood looks like for children with disabilities, one joyful ride at a time.

(MKRO Kindness Grant Winner, Jan 2024)

> **Reflections:** Aanand shows us that creativity and compassion can open new worlds of independence and joy for kids facing big challenges. Who is a kindness hero in your life, and how can you honor them?

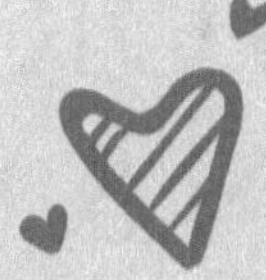

We spend precious hours fearing the inevitable. It would be wise to use that time adoring our families, cherishing our friends, and living our lives.

– Maya Angelou

RESTORING WOMEN'S VOICES

When Simon Emmanuel Mollel was a boy in Orkeeswa Village, Tanzania, he often watched his mother rise before the sun. While most of the world was still sleeping, she was already busy with the endless work of fetching water, tending goats, and preparing food. She carried the weight of her family's survival on her shoulders, yet she had no say in the family's future. Simon remembers standing quietly in the doorway, watching her bend over a cooking fire, her face illuminated by its glow. She was strong, determined, and deeply loving, but he could also see the exhaustion in her eyes.

What broke his heart wasn't the work. It was the injustice. No matter how hard she worked, her voice didn't count. She had no rights to the land she tilled, no say in the decisions that shaped her life, no real freedom to dream. "I remember thinking as a child," Simon said softly, "'One day, I will change this. One day, I will bring back happiness to women like my mother.'"

That promise became the heartbeat of Simon's life. After his mother passed away in 2012, the injustice he had witnessed only became clearer. He saw other women in his Maasai community enduring the same struggles: widows cast aside without support, girls forced into early marriages, women suffering from domestic abuse, or subjected to female genital mutilation. Their silence wasn't a choice, it was enforced by generations of tradition that never gave them a seat at the table.

In 2021, Simon decided it was time to stop waiting for change and start building it. He founded the Nadumu Maasai Women's Organization. "Nadumu" means "develop" or "maintain" in Swahili, and its mission is to give women the tools to reclaim dignity, independence, and hope.

One of NMW's earliest projects was simple but powerful: helping widows and single mothers start small businesses. A group of women sat together weaving beaded table mats, their hands moving steadily as they traded stories and laughter filled the space. Others raised chickens, selling eggs at the market, learning how to save and reinvest their earnings.

It wasn't just about money. It was about the possibility.

Simon still remembers delivering the organization's first supply of sanitary pads to a school of young girls. One girl clutched the package tightly, her expression full of quiet relief. In that moment, Simon imagined what she might be thinking, that now she could stay in school every day. Something as small as a pad meant she no longer had to miss classes each month out of shame or lack of resources. It meant dignity, opportunity, and a future.

Under Simon's leadership, NMW has helped establish community banking systems, donated pens to over 2,000 children, and planted 1,000 trees to combat devastating soil erosion. But the most meaningful change is harder to measure: it's in the way women now gather, sit side by side, and speak. They share burdens. They plan futures. They dare to imagine lives filled with freedom, education, and respect.

"Working together allows women to see they are not alone," Simon explained. "It gives them strength, resilience, and hope."

The ripple effect is undeniable. The women Simon supports become role models for their daughters and leaders in their villages. They carry with them the quiet but powerful truth that change isn't just possible, it's already happening.

As the first international recipient of the MKRO Kindness Grant, Simon embodies the courage and compassion that can transform entire communities. His story began with one boy watching his mother's silent struggle, but it has grown into a movement that restores voices, rights, and dreams to women across Tanzania.

Simon still thinks often of his mother. In every business started, in every girl who stays in school, in every tree planted, he feels he is keeping the promise he made as a boy: to bring back her happiness by making sure no woman's voice is silenced again.

(MKRO Kindness Grant Winner, Mar 2024)

> **Reflections:** Simon uses the power of standing up for those who are often unheard, using compassion and community to uplift women and create lasting change. What role does kindness play in forgiveness and second chances?

*I learned the most about the value
of ordinary from interviewing men
and women who have experienced
tremendous loss, such as the loss
of a child, violence, genocide, and
trauma. The memories that they
held most sacred were the ordinary,
everyday moments. It was clear that
their most precious memories were
forged from a collection of ordinary
moments, and their hope for others
is that they would stop long enough
to be grateful for those moments and
the joy they bring.*

– Brene Brown

KINDNESS IN EVERY BASKET

When the little boy spotted the basket waiting on his bed, his eyes widened. Inside were bright beach toys, a soft blanket, sunscreen, and a book bursting with color. He ran his hands over the items, pulling each one out with a kind of reverence, as if he couldn't believe they were meant for him. His mother, watching from the doorway, was doing that thing that parents do when they're trying very hard not to cry. After months of hospital corridors, medical tests, and way too many sleepless nights, this small thoughtful surprise felt like a lifeline.

That basket didn't magically appear. It was packed with love by a teenager named Jude Al-Hamad.

Jude, from Berlin, Maryland, was already juggling AP classes, family life, and volunteer work, basically the full high-school overachiever schedule. But when she learned about the struggles facing children with critical illnesses and their families, she couldn't let it go. Onc question kept nudging her: What can I do to help?

Her search led her to the Believe in Tomorrow Children's Foundation whose mission is beautifully simple and deeply needed: keep families together during treatment by offering free overnight accommodations near hospitals, along with respite homes at the beach and in the mountains. For families living under the constant strain of illness, these homes offer something priceless, rest, laughter, and a moment to breathe. Their mission resonated deeply with Jude.

When Jude realized one of the respite homes was right in her own beach community, she knew she had found her way to make a difference. She organized fundraisers, rallied support, and raised over $1,000 worth of summer necessities for the children and families who would stay there.

As her senior year approached and college loomed ahead, Jude wanted to leave behind something more personal, something that carried her love in every detail. So she applied for and received a MKRO Kindness Grant. With it, she set out to create individualized care baskets for the families staying at the Believe in Tomorrow respite home.

For weeks, Jude poured herself into the project. She thought about what would make a child smile after a hard day, or what small comfort could ease a parent's load. Each item was chosen with care, each basket arranged to feel less like a gift and more like a hug.

When the baskets were finally delivered, the reactions said it all, kids laughing as they explored their treasures, parents offering tearful thanks. For Jude, it was confirmation that kindness isn't abstract; it's lived, felt, and remembered in moments like these.

Reflecting on the experience, Jude shared, "It was so heart-warming and fun to make these baskets. As I've told you before, I've done collection drives for Believe in Tomorrow before, but this time, making these care packages felt extra special. There is no way to describe all the love and kindness I've felt ever since you told me I won the MKRO grant."

Her words capture what so many discover when they choose kindness: it nourishes the giver as deeply as the receiver.

One teenage girl, a handful of baskets, and the ripple continues.

(MKRO Kindness Grant Winner, Feb 2019)

Reflections: Jude's compassion teaches us that kindness not only helps others but also fills the giver with joy and purpose. What's one intentional act you could do this week to pass that joy forward to someone else?

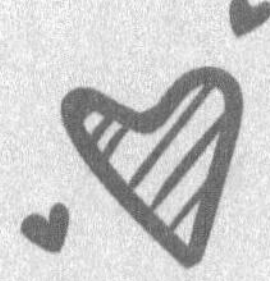

Choosing to have joy is not naively thinking everything will be easy. It is courageously believing that there is still hope, even when things get hard.

– Morgan Harper Nichols

CREATING BELONGING THROUGH SOCCER

The boy stood off to the side, watching other kids race across the soccer field. His shoes were too small, his T-shirt hung loose at the neck, and though his eyes followed every move of the ball, he didn't step forward. When a coach waved him over, his first thought wasn't "Yay!" It was, "I can't, I don't belong here."

That moment stayed with Kaig Lightner. Mostly because he was that kid once. The hesitation, the fear of rejection, the heavy weight of feeling like an outsider. And right then, it became the seed of something bigger. He thought, what if there was a soccer club where no child ever had to wonder if they belonged?

So in 2013, after months of scraping together seed money, writing grant proposals, and calling in every favor imaginable, including getting donated gear from Nike, Kaig launched Portland Community Football Club. The club came with one beautifully radical rule: nobody gets cut. Ever. The registration fee was only $50, but if families couldn't pay, it didn't matter. Kids played anyway. End of discussion.

This wasn't just about soccer. For kids from immigrant families living in Portland's most under-resourced neighborhoods, opportunities like this were rare. PCFC gave them more than a team; it gave them a community. It gave them someone in their corner. Families quickly learned that the club didn't just provide uniforms and cleats; it also helped with groceries, rent assistance, and connecting them to critical social services. Basically, if life got hard, as it often does, PCFC showed up.

Kaig understood what these kids were carrying. Growing up, he had been bullied, called names, and made to feel like a "freak" for being different. Soccer saved him. It was the place where the noise of the world faded and he could just be. "Soccer had been my main way of finding healing and connection, and I wanted that for these kids, too," Kaig says.

But while he poured himself into making a safe space for others, Kaig was holding back part of his own story. He is transgender, born female, and for years he worried that sharing that truth would cost him the trust of his players and their families. So he stayed quiet. Until he didn't.

When Kaig finally chose honesty, he told his players about growing up feeling unseen, about the loneliness of not fitting in, about the courage it took to become who he really was.

One of his earliest players, Shema Jacques, remembers that day vividly. "Suddenly, hearing that, it all made sense," Shema said. "This is why he knows what it's like for so many of us, not being accepted, trying hard to fit in. I felt more connected to him, and I realized I am not alone. He was still the person I looked up to and wanted to be like."

Instead of losing trust, Kaig's honesty drew his community closer. The families didn't walk away; they embraced him even more. His vulnerability became the foundation of something stronger: a team built not just on skill, but on courage, kindness, and belonging.

Today, PCFC has grown to three hundred and fifty-five players, with more coaches and a small staff. But the heart of the program is still the same: every child belongs. And every kid knows that the person teaching them how to pass and shoot is also teaching them how to show up as their full honest self and how to extend compassion to others.

The boy who once thought "I don't belong here" found his place on the field. And because of Kaig's vision, countless other kids have, too.

(MKRO Kindness Grant Winner, Jul 2024)

> **Reflections:** Kaig shows us that courage and authenticity can create safe spaces where everyone belongs and feels supported. How can we extend kindness to people who are different from us?

*You can choose what you stand for
and what you will try to accomplish.
You can choose, when hopes and
fears are swirling in your head,
to clutch at hope. Amid beauty
and ugliness, to fasten on beauty.
Between despair and possibility,
to pursue the possible. Of love and
hate, to opt for love. These are choices
entirely in your power to make.*

– David Von Drehle

SPREADING SMILES ONE EPISODE AT A TIME

When Robert Peterpaul thinks about kindness, he doesn't picture some big, abstract concept you'd find on a motivational poster; he thinks about a dimly lit hospital room, the steady hum of machines, and the unexpected magic that movies brought into it. Robert was just a kid, sitting beside his younger brother Thomas, who was bravely battling cancer. The days were long and heavy, the air filled with antiseptic smells and way too much waiting. But when a movie flickered on the screen, everything changed. For a little while, Thomas wasn't a patient, he was just a kid laughing, dreaming, and escaping.

And then something extraordinary began to happen: the stars of those films reached back. Sylvester Stallone and Angelina Jolie sent signed photos with words of encouragement. And Steven Tyler, from the band Aerosmith, went full rock legend and brought Thomas onstage during a concert. One moment, one kid, pure joy. No hospital gowns, no IV poles, just a memory that would last forever.

For Robert, those gestures changed everything. "It wasn't just the celebrity," he says. "It was the feeling that my brother mattered. That people saw him and wanted to lift his spirit." Those moments became lifelines for the whole family, reminders that they weren't alone in the hardest season of their lives.

Thomas didn't survive his illness. But the kindness that surrounded him left an indelible mark on Robert. "Witnessing what my brother went through, and all the acts of kindness we subsequently received from our community, has made spreading kindness my lifelong mission and religion of sorts," he says.

To honor Thomas's memory, Robert and his family created The Thomas Peterpaul Foundation. Over the years, the foundation has supported pediatric cancer patients and their families in moments when hope feels hard to hold on to. They've raised awareness about childhood cancer, provided emotional and financial support, and helped fund critical medical research. Robert even found himself testifying before Congress alongside Novartis, advocating for CAR T-cell therapy, a breakthrough treatment now saving children's lives.

But Robert's mission didn't stop there. He wanted to spread the feeling, the kind that made a hospital room feel lighter, far beyond the walls of a medical center. That's when he launched The Art of Kindness, a podcast devoted to shining a light on goodness in the world, especially in the arts.

Each week, Robert sits down with actors, musicians, Broadway stars, and other creatives who use their platforms to make a difference. The conversations are warm and real, filled with laughter, tears, and a deep sense of humanity. Guests like

Meghan Trainor, Lin-Manuel Miranda, and the legendary Carol Burnett have shared their own philosophies on kindness. Carol Burnett put it simply: "Just don't hurt anyone's feelings." That one sentence, Robert believes, is the perfect reminder that kindness doesn't have to be complicated; it can be woven into the smallest choices we make every day.

Producing the podcast takes time, energy, and heart, but Robert shows up every week with the same intention: that someone listening will feel a little less alone, a little more seen, and a little more inspired to choose kindness themselves.

What began as a deeply personal response to loss has grown into a movement that touches lives far beyond Robert's own. Through his foundation and his podcast, he keeps his brother's spirt alive in the most beautiful way, by making sure kindness never stops rippling outward.

Supporting Robert's work means believing in that ripple effect. It means holding onto the truth that small acts, multiplied, can change the world. And it means honoring the legacy of a boy named Thomas, who inspired his big brother to spread kindness like confetti, one story at a time.

(MKRO Kindness Grant Winner, Sept 2024)

Reflection: Robert shows us that kindness can live in creativity, conversation, and storytelling. What's one area of your life where you'd like to grow in kindness?

We tend to remember the dramatic incidents that change history – Armstrong's walk on the moon, Nixon's resignation, and the Loma Prieta earthquake, but we live for the quiet, intimate moments that mark not our calendars but our hearts.

– Robert Dugoni

PLANTING HOPE

When a teenager named Malik showed up at Southside Blooms for his first day of work, he didn't say much. He kept his hood pulled low, hands shoved deep into his pockets, eyes darting to the ground. He had seen too much in his short life: friends lost to violence, dreams shut down by poverty, and a neighborhood that seemed to offer nothing but dead ends. When someone handed him a trowel and pointed to a patch of dirt, Malik gave a look that clearly said, *You've got to be kidding me.*

But a few hours later, there he was, kneeling in the soil, gently pressing sunflower seeds into the ground. And something shifted. For the first time in a long while, someone had trusted him with life instead of expecting him to destroy it. Turns out, that changes a person.

That's the quiet, radical power of Southside Blooms, the nonprofit founded by Quilen and Hannah Blackwell. What started in 2014 with a humble $150 donation has become a network of solar-powered flower farms transforming vacant lots across Chicago's South and West Sides. Places once known for neglect and loss now burst with color, rows of dahlias, roses, and sunflowers tended by young people who had been written off far too soon.

Southside Blooms doesn't just plant flowers; it plants purpose. Teenagers like Malik learn to grow and harvest blossoms, care for bees and chickens, and even design wedding bouquets. They earn paychecks, sure, but more importantly, they discover that their work has value. "When people buy these flowers for their most important celebrations, weddings, anniversaries, birthdays, it tells our youth that something they created is worth cherishing," Quilen explains. That's a powerful message, especially when the world has been telling you the opposite.

Quilen never set out to be a flower farmer. Raised in Madison, Wisconsin, with two parents in corporate jobs, he never worried about food on the table or safety in his neighborhood. Poverty wasn't part of his daily reality, until he joined the Peace Corps and lived in rural villages overseas. Seeing hardship up close changed him. Later, while mentoring high school students in Chicago and listening to their stories of fear and loss, it hit him just how easily his life could've gone another way. "I felt God gripping my heart," he recalls. "I knew I could either use my blessings for myself, or I could use them to serve."

With Hannah by his side, Quilen began dreaming of a social enterprise that could chip away at systemic poverty. Flowers seemed unlikely at first, fragile, temporary things. But the more they thought about it, the more it made sense. Flowers are joy made visible. They soften hard places. They remind us that beauty can grow where no one expects it.

Today, Southside Blooms runs six farms and two flower shop, one in North Lawndale and one in Englewood, among Chicago's toughest neighborhoods. Where abandoned lots once stood, bees now hum and sunflowers reach for the sky.

Kids who might have been swallowed up by street violence now walk home with dirt under their nails and pride in their eyes.

"As strange as it sounds, we believe flowers can save lives," Quilen says. "They give kids a reason to choose the shop over the street. They show the world that the Black community has brilliance and beauty to share."

Quilen and Hannah remind us that the smallest seeds, when planted in faith and watered with kindness, can grow into something strong enough to change lives.

(MKRO Kindness Award Winner, Apr 2024)

> **Reflection:** Flowers may seem small, but in Quilen and Hannah's hands, they have become tools of transformation. Who has shown you kindness that shaped who you are today? Let them know the impact that had on your life.

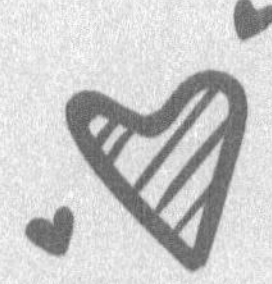

There are two components that are fundamental to enjoy life and feel good about yourself: continual learning and service to others.

– Tim Ferriss

HEARTS OF KINDNESS

When Neel Sood walked into his fourth-grade classroom at Hamilton Primary School one morning, he noticed something that didn't sit right with him. A few of his classmates sat quietly at their desks, heads down, while others whispered about who was "cool" and who wasn't. At just nine years old, Neel could see what many adults overlook: some kids were already feeling left out, invisible, or like they didn't matter. And Neel wasn't having it.

A simple thought popped into his head: What if everyone had a reminder that they were special? What if kindness wasn't just something you said but something you could actually hold in your hands?

From that moment, Neel began what would become the Hearts of Kindness Project.

Armed with stacks of colorful paper, scissors, markers, and more determination than most grown-ups, Neel got to work at his dining room table. He cut heart after heart, carefully decorated each one and attached a small card with a message meant to lift spirits. Some were simple truths he believed in, like "It's cool to be kind" or "If you think someone could use a friend, be one." Others came straight from his own imagination, all chosen with one reason: to remind people they matter.

On the back of each heart, Neel added his favorite part: "Write your superpower on your heart." He wanted every kid to pause and think about what made them special, not just students in desks, but as heroes-in-the-making with something important to offer the world.

This was no small project. Neel made over four hundred and seventy hearts, one for every single student at Hamilton School. He even used his own birthday money to buy the supplies, which might be the most impressive thing any nine-year-old has ever done with birthday cash.

The day he handed them out was magic. Classrooms filled with color, chatter, and laughter. Kids began reading their messages aloud, sharing their "superpowers," and seeing each other a little differently. Neel noticed a girl who usually kept to herself, clutching her heart tightly, her face softening as if, for the first time, she felt truly seen. Nearby, a boy who was usually restless and distracted sat a little taller, his grin wide, as though he had just discovered that his gift for making people laugh was something to be proud of.

What started as a simple craft project turned into a wave of connection. Teachers noticed the difference, too. Kids were kinder to one another, more inclusive, more willing to speak words of encouragement. The school felt brighter, not because of the decorations, but because of the new spirit filling the halls.

Neel's idea didn't stay within the school walls. His project was featured on the school's website and in the local paper, inspiring others in the community. But for Neel, it wasn't about recognition. He was already dreaming of where kindness could go next. His next stop: a local nursing home, where he hopes to deliver handmade hearts to residents who may feel forgotten, bringing them the same spark of joy he shared with his classmates.

Neel reminds us that kindness isn't complicated, and it doesn't take a lifetime to start. It can begin with paper, scissors, and a little imagination. More importantly, it can begin with the choice of one child who looks at the world and decides to make it better.

Because of Neel, hundreds of children walk through their school days with a heart in their hand and kindness on their mind. And that is how change begins, one small heart at a time.

(MKRO Kindness Award Winner, Jun 2024)

> **Reflections:** Neel shows us that even the smallest acts of kindness, like a handmade heart or kind words, can spread joy and make everyone feel valued and special. How do you feel when you choose kindness, even in small ways?

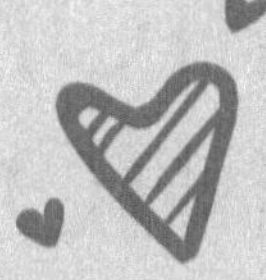

Be kind. You will remember when you weren't. How you treat other people will bring you either peace or despair as you age, and it will certainly impact how you are remembered after you die.

– Diane Button

CHAMPIONS FOR SENIORS

When Jerry Martin and Elaine Mack step into a senior mobile home park in Mesa, Arizona, they aren't just visitors; they're lifelines. One afternoon, they met a woman in her late seventies who was sitting outside in the brutal desert heat because her air conditioner had broken down. She had no money to fix it and no family nearby to help. The desert sun can be cruel, and for someone her age, it was more than uncomfortable. It was dangerous. Jerry didn't hesitate. He rolled up his sleeves. Elaine made some calls, and by that evening the woman's AC was humming again. She cried as she thanked them, not just because of the cool air, but because for the first time in weeks, she felt like someone saw her.

That is the kind of quiet, everyday heroism Jerry and Elaine embody. Retired themselves, they could be spending their golden years golfing, traveling, or perfecting the art of afternoon naps. Instead, they've made it their mission to stand beside Arizona's most vulnerable seniors, people living in low-income

55+ communities, many of whom are only one rent increase, one medical bill, or one broken appliance away from crisis.

It's staggering to realize that more than 17 million Americans over the age of sixty-five live with economic insecurity. For seniors living just above the poverty line, a single unexpected expense can mean the difference between stability and desperation. These are the people Jerry and Elaine serve, neighbors who might otherwise fall through the cracks.

On most days, you'll find them in community rooms or shaded outdoor spaces, teaching seniors about their rights under the Landlord Tenant Act for mobile homeowners, laws that are too often ignored by landowners. They explain how to fight unfair rent hikes, how to access utility assistance, and how to keep food on the table. And if talking isn't enough, they act. If someone doesn't have groceries, they deliver food. If an electric bill is overdue, they step in to help. And when housing becomes impossible to afford, they work tirelessly to find safe alternatives so no one ends up homeless.

And here's the part that really gets you: much of this comes straight out of their own pockets. Gas money, food deliveries, the phone calls, and the hours upon hours of time. They even started a food bank so no senior ever has to choose between paying for medicine and eating dinner.

When asked why they do it, Jerry shrugs and says: "We were raised right. We don't think of ourselves when helping others; it just comes naturally." Elaine smiles and adds that the real reward is seeing fear lift off someone's shoulders when they realize they're not alone.

To the seniors they help, Jerry and Elaine aren't just advocates, they're protectors, mentors, and trusted friends. They bring dignity back into lives that the world too often overlooks.

It's impossible to measure the ripple effect of their compassion, but you can see it in the grateful tears of a senior who can finally cool down, in the laughter at a community gathering where hope feels possible again, and in the quiet strength of a senior who knows someone has their back.

Jerry and Elaine never ask for recognition, and honestly, they'd probably brush it off if you tried. But their work speaks louder than any award ever could. They remind us that two people with empathy and determination can move mountains, or at the very least, keep a roof overhead, food on the table, and hope alive.

They are, without question, unsung heroes. And because of them, the seniors of Arizona are safer, stronger, and less alone.

(MKRO Kindness Award Winner, Aug 2024)

Reflections: Jerry and Elaine show us that unwavering dedication and compassion can create real hope and dignity. If someone described you as kind, what would you want that to mean?

Character isn't fate or destiny. Character isn't DNA, decided before birth. Character is the result of your little choices and little actions.

– Derek Sivers

CARRYING LOVE, NOT TRASH BAGS

When the phone rang that afternoon, Amanda Durante wasn't expecting her life to change. On the other end was her close friend, social worker Samantha Nurmenniemi, her voice heavy with the kind of exhaustion that comes from seeing too much heartbreak. Samantha explained that children entering foster care in her area were showing up with nothing but the clothes on their backs. "Sometimes," she said, "they come in carrying trash bags with whatever they could grab. That's it."

Amanda sat with the image, small hands gripping a crinkled trash bag, a child's entire world stuffed inside like discarded belongings. For Amanda, who had endured her own difficult childhood, the thought hit especially hard. She couldn't shake it. "No child should ever feel like their life fits into a garbage bag," she thought. And instead of saying, "That's awful," or "I'm so sorry," Amanda did what kindness heroes do best. Her first words back to Samantha were: "How can I help? What can we build?"

That single question became the seed of The Wandering Heart Project, a grassroots organization Amanda and Samantha launched that day to provide foster children and children experiencing homelessness with dignity, comfort, and care. What they didn't expect was just how quickly the need would reveal itself.

The numbers alone are staggering: more than 1.6 million children experience homelessness every year in the U.S., and over 442,000 are in foster care. Many of these children arrive without pajamas, without a toothbrush, and little more than fear in their eyes. They are shuffled from place to place, sometimes moving ten or fifteen times before adulthood. That kind of instability leaves marks.

But numbers don't tell the whole story. Like the little boy who had been removed from a dangerous home in the middle of the night arrived at a shelter in socks and an oversized T-shirt, shivering and confused. That's who The Wandering Heart Project shows up for, by delivering a suitcase filled with clothes in his size: warm pajamas, a soft hoodie, sneakers that fit, and a stuffed animal tucked in the side pocket.

Moments like that fuel Amanda and Samantha's work. They refuse to hand over "good enough" donations. Every child receives five to seven thoughtfully chosen outfits, brand-new socks and underwear, toiletries, and always a suitcase or duffel bag, never a trash bag. In winter, coats and gloves are added. In summer, swimsuits and flip-flops. Each package carries a simple but powerful message: You matter. You deserve care. You are not forgotten.

Word spread quickly. One Facebook post asking for donations turned into hundreds of messages within days. Bags of new clothes appeared on porches, boxes arrived in the mail, and volunteers offered to sort and deliver. In their first year, the Wandering Heart Project supported more than 500 children across Massachusetts, from newborns to young adults.

For Amanda, each delivery is personal. She sees herself in the children, the uncertainty in their eyes, the weight of feeling unwanted. By giving kids not just essentials, but items chosen with dignity and love, she hopes they feel what she once longed for: safety, worth, and belonging.

Though Amanda was nominated for recognition, she insists this is a two-person story. "It wouldn't exist without Samantha," she says. And she's right. Their partnership is proof of what happens when compassion refuses to sit still.

Children who once carried trash bags now carry suitcases filled with care. And tucked inside each one is something even more powerful than clothing: hope.

(MKRO Kindness Award Winner, Oct 2024)

> **Reflection:** Amanda shows us that compassion combined with action can transform people's lives. When was the last time someone's kindness made a lasting impact on you?

If you planted hope today in a heart that felt alone, if you caused a laugh that chased away some tears, if someone's burden was made lighter because of your kindness, your day was well spent.

– Unknown

FIGHTING FOR THEIR FUTURE

When a shy, thirteen-year-old boy first walked into New Jersey Give a Kid a Dream (NJGAKAD) in Long Branch, he carried more than a backpack on his shoulders. He carried the weight of being bullied at school, the fear of disappointing his single mother, and that quiet, heartbreaking belief that maybe his life wouldn't amount to much. He avoided eye contact, shuffled his feet, and mumbled when spoken to. Then Jackie Atkins stepped in, tied gloves on his hands, looked him straight in the eye and said, "You belong here."

That small moment, someone seeing him, naming him as worthy, changed everything. And it's this kind of moment that Jackie has been creating for kids over and over again through NJGAKAD, the after-school program she founded to give children from underserved communities more than boxing skills. Yes, they learn how to throw a punch, but more importantly, they learn how to stand tall when life throws one first.

Jackie knows firsthand what it means to fight through adversity. A former world boxing champion and member of the New Jersey Boxing Hall of Fame, she left a successful corporate career to devote herself fully to coaching, but her vision has always gone beyond the ring. For her, boxing is just the doorway. The real goal is to raise young people who believe in themselves, who can withstand life's blows with resilience, and who can imagine a future filled with possibility.

Step into the gym on a weekday afternoon, and you'll plenty of jabs and hooks, but you'll also see kids hunched over homework at the side of the ring because Jackie insists education comes first. You'll hear laughter during lessons on how to shake hands firmly, look someone in the eye, or set the table for a five-course meal, a skill most never dreamed they'd need until Jackie brought them to Buona Sera Ristorante and showed them that, yes, they belong at every table.

One of Jackie's proudest trips was to Fighter's Heaven, Muhammad Ali's legendary training camp. Standing where Ali once trained, Jackie told her students, "Greatness isn't just about what you win, it's about who you are, how you give, how you rise when life knocks you down." Those words stick because they come from someone who lives them daily.

Her programs, like Champions of Life, which helps kids face bullying, and Girls in Gloves, which teaches self-defense while building confidence and self-worth, meets her students where they are. For many, the gym becomes their safe place, a second home. "Once they come here, you can see a peace come over them," says board member Alicia Furman.

And the kids themselves tell the story best. Anthony Micciulli, who once struggled with depression, says, "Give A Kid A Dream and boxing in general have had a huge impact on my life. I went from being a kid who was severely depressed and upset all the time to having multiple sponsorships and being very successful. I want to thank Coach Jackie because she changed my life and molded me into the man I am today."

Jackie isn't just building fighters, she's building futures. With every glove she ties, every word of encouragement, and every moment of tough love, she's reminding kids of something powerful: you are stronger than you think, and you matter more than you know.

(MKRO Kindness Grant Winner, Nov 2024)

> **Reflection:** Jackie's story reminds us that mentorship and opportunity can open doors that young people never knew existed. Do you believe kindness is more powerful than criticism? Why or why not?

Your brain is a supercomputer, and your self-talk is the program it will run. Positive or negative is up to you.

– Jim Kwik

THE MAD HATTER PROJECT

They say if you want to quiet your mind, step into nature. For Curtis Jones that has always meant hiking Mt Sanitas in Boulder, Colorado.

At first glance, Mt. Sanitas looks like just another mountain trail, steep in places, a good workout for the legs and lungs, with a spectacular view of Boulder from the summit. But for Curtis, it became something deeper, a lifeline.

At the height of the pandemic, when the world was unraveling and Curtis was facing both professional and personal storms, Mt. Sanitas became his therapy. Reaching the top, Curtis would often remind himself of something his geologist dad might have said: "This mountain will still be here in ten thousand years."

That thought grounded him. The pain he was carrying felt smaller up there, real, but temporary. And that perspective helped him breathe again.

What started as personal healing quietly turned outward. While hiking Blackett's Ridge in Tucson, Curtis noticed someone wearing a hat embroidered with the name of the trail. He loved it and bought one, but the idea kept tugging at him. What if he made hats for Mt. Sanitas? Not to sell, but to give away.

And so, the Mt Sanitas Mad Hatter Project was born.

He designed a breathable cap with "Mt. Sanitas Boulder, Colorado" stitched on the front and its elevation, "6,863 feet," on the side. He ordered 25 and began carrying them in his backpack, offering them to fellow hikers along the trail.

The first hat he gave away, he knew he was onto something. The woman looked at the hat, eyes brimming, and said, "No one has ever randomly given me something this nice for free. It feels like Christmas in the summer."

Curtis ordered more, 25 then 50, then hundreds. Even supply delays didn't stop him. To date he has given away more than 1,250 hats. And with each one came a story.

"At first, giving out these caps was just a kind gesture." Curtis said. "What I've realized is the Mt. Sanitas Mad Hatter Project isn't about the hat. It's about the brief moments of human connection in a world that's incredibly complicated and often moves too fast. It's a reminder that kindness is the best of what humans can be."

On the trail, people open up. Curtis has listened to stories of job loss, divorce, grief, identity shifts, and fresh starts. One day, after giving hats to two women at the trailhead, one shared through tears that she was part of Boulder's Jewish community, still reeling from a recent attack on peaceful protesters. Curtis carried that moment with him long after the hike ended.

Something else unexpected happened, too: community. Strangers started recognizing each other by the hat. Friendships formed. A quiet web of connection began to grow, all tied together by a simple act of generosity.

Not just anyone handing out hats on the mountain would create this kind of ripple. The magic of the Mad Hatter Project is Curtis himself, his open, nonjudgmental heart, his easy smile, his genuine curiosity about people. He listens without trying to fix or judge. People feel safe with him, and that's why these moments land so deeply.

If you find yourself hiking Mt. Sanitas one day and someone offers you a cap, accept it. Share what the mountain means to you. And know that behind that simple gift is something far greater: a reminder that small, ordinary acts can change the course of someone's day, or even their life.

And if you're inspired, pay it forward in your own way. Hold the door open. Write a kind note. Smile at a stranger. Let kindness ripple on.

(MKRO Kindness Award Winner, Dec 2025)

> **Reflections:** Curtis reminds us that kindness can be as simple as showing up, paying attention, and offering a small gesture that says, I see you and you're not alone. What is one small gesture you can do on a regular basis to put kindness out in our world?

To make a difference in someone's life you don't have to be brilliant, rich, beautiful or perfect. You just have to care.

– Mandy Hale

LEADING WITH HEART

I t was just before Thanksgiving when Linda McGean walked through the cafeteria at Ocean City Elementary School and noticed what many might have overlooked. Some children sat laughing with friends, but others pushed food around their trays, their faces clouded with worries far too heavy for their age. Linda always sees them, the quiet signs of struggle, the children trying to make themselves small, the ones carrying burdens no child should have to bear. She never calls attention to them in a way that would embarrass them, but she makes a quiet note to herself, already thinking of how she can help.

By that evening, she had set things in motion. Quietly, without seeking recognition, Linda organized collections of food, clothing, school supplies, and gift cards, whatever was needed most. Families who might have gone without found essentials waiting for them, often delivered discreetly so children could feel secure and cared for. For Linda, it wasn't just about meeting immediate needs; it was about restoring dignity and hope, making sure every child and family knew they weren't alone.

This is what Linda McGean does every single day. Officially, she is the school counselor at Ocean City Elementary School in Ocean City, MD. Unofficially, she is the school's heartbeat, the mentor, cheerleader, counselor, organizer, and champion for every student and staff member who passes through the doors. With a permanent smile and an encouraging word, she embodies compassion in action.

Her influence is woven into the fabric of the school. Teachers lean on her when they're having a hard day, students seek her out when they feel unseen, and families know that if they hit a rough patch, Linda will be there with resources, encouragement, and open arms. Her colleagues often remark that you never hear a negative word from her, only words that build you up, words that make you feel capable of facing whatever comes next.

One of her proudest creations is the Stand Up Speak Up program, which promotes positive personality traits throughout the year. Each month, a new theme: kindness, empathy, respect, responsibility, becomes the focus. In September, the school kicks off with kindness: pep rallies that fill the gym with cheers, classroom lessons that spark real conversations, and daily reminders from Linda that kindness isn't a one-time act but a way of living. Under her leadership, these aren't just abstract ideas; they become habits. They become culture.

And when life gets hard for a student or a family, Linda is the first to step in. Food, clothing, shelter, school supplies, she mobilizes it all, often before others even know there's a need. She does it quietly, never asking for credit, always directing the attention back to the dignity of the people she helps.

Her advocacy is fierce but tender. If a child doesn't have a voice, Linda becomes their voice. If a child feels invisible, Linda makes sure they are seen. If a child doubts their worth, she reminds them, again and again, that they matter.

Her example continues to ripple outward, reminding us that real change begins with noticing, the child sitting alone, the family struggling silently, and then stepping in with love.

Linda doesn't just guide her students through school. She gives them the gift of knowing that someone believes in them, always. And sometimes, that belief is the very thing that changes the course of a life.

(MKRO Kindness Award Winner, Nov 2019)

Reflections: Linda shows us that kindness is about being a constant source of encouragement, support, and hope. What is one small act of kindness you could do for a neighbor, friend, or stranger today? Write it down and commit to making it happen.

The people I've spent significant time with at the end of their lives, do not talk about their degrees, promotions, or having successfully kept their weight down. They talk about the times and places of love. Loving memories are the fields in which we walk with them near the end.

– Anne Lamott

A LIFE WOVEN WITH KINDNESS AND PURPOSE

Jennie Bouchard-Young knows what it means to miss someone so deeply it aches. As a child in foster care, she was separated from her siblings, left to wonder where they were, if they were safe, and when, if ever, she might see them again. That kind of ache doesn't go away easily. It settles in, becomes part of who you are. But instead of letting that pain make her hard or bitter she turned it into a vow: no child should have to grow up believing that family bonds could be broken beyond repair.

That vow became the seed for something extraordinary. Jennie helped bring Camp to Belong to Maine, a program designed to reunite siblings separated by foster care. It was her vision, born from her own heartbreak, that brothers and sisters deserved a space to laugh, play, and simply be family again. For many children, it was the first time in years they had been able to hug each other, share stories, or just sit side by side without the pain of separation between them. For Jennie, it was proof that kindness could transform pain into something profoundly beautiful.

Jennie's journey began long before the camp. As a teenager, she stepped into advocacy work to help improve Maine's foster care system. She wanted those still inside it to feel seen and supported and to know someone was fighting for them.

Later, in her twenties, she worked at a group home for children, pouring her heart into making sure every young person felt valued and worthy of love. She didn't see it as a job; she saw it as a calling. Every hug, every encouraging word, every moment of patience was a message she wished someone had given her younger self.

Jennie has found creative outlets, too: she taught herself to knit so she could make scarves for Operation Gratitude, sending warmth and care to American troops and veterans. She's knitted hundreds of hats for newborns and cancer patients, all self-funded, and started projects like Knitting Love for a Cause and the Kindness Ducks Project, where she leaves uplifting posters, sticky notes, or tokens of encouragement in public spaces. At Arlington National Cemetery, she's handed out star pins and notes to veterans, reminding them they are not forgotten.

What makes Jennie extraordinary isn't just the sheer volume of what she gives; it's the heart behind it all. Every gesture comes from a place of lived experience, from a woman who knows what it means to feel lonely and who has dedicated her life to making sure others never feel that way.

Jennie has turned her hardest chapters into a lifelong ripple of kindness. She reminds us that pain doesn't have to define us; it can refine us. That resilience can grow into compassion. And that sometimes the smallest acts, a knitted hat, a handwritten note, a week at camp, can change everything.

(MKRO Kindness Award Winner, Jun 2025)

Reflection: Jennie's story reminds us that our hardships don't have to harden us; they can become the very fuel for compassion. How might you take something difficult from your past and transform it into a source of kindness for others?

We have no idea what tomorrow will bring, but today is overflowing with potential.

– Allan Lokos

LIGHT IN DARK PLACES

Sarah Shelke was only thirteen when she first understood what it meant to feel powerless. Her older brother, the one who made her laugh, and helped with homework, had fallen into a darkness she didn't understand. His laughter grew rare. His bedroom door stayed shut. Dinner became quiet, heavy with unspoken worry. Sarah remembers wishing she could do something, anything, to bring him back.

That experience changed her. It wasn't just watching her brother struggle with depression; it was realizing that so many young people were silently fighting the same battles with no support. She thought about her classmates, the ones who looked fine on the outside but might be breaking inside. She thought about how often kids hear "you'll be okay" when what they really need is help, resources, and someone who truly understands.

So Sarah did the one thing she could: she opened her phone. She created a simple Instagram page where teens could see posts about stress, self-care, and encouragement. No grand plan, no funding, just heart. She hoped it might reach a handful of people, maybe a few friends would see it and feel a little less alone.

But then something wild happened. Messages started pouring in and not just from friends, but from teens across the country. Kids saying, "I finally feel seen." Others admitting they'd been too scared to talk to anyone in their lives but found comfort in her words.

That's when Sarah realized awareness wasn't enough. Her heart ached reading those messages because it wasn't just her brother; it was thousands of young people. She decided right then, she didn't just want to post about mental health, she wanted to do something about it. So, at fifteen, she founded Mind4Youth, a nonprofit focused on giving young people the tools, mentors, and community they need to take care of their mental health.

What began as a social media account quickly grew into a global movement that now reaches thousands of teens across forty-seven countries. Through Mind4Youth, Sarah organizes workshops on stress management, coping strategies, and breaking down stigma. She created a mentorship program that pairs high school students with trained college mentors, because sometimes what a teenager needs most is someone just a few steps ahead to say, I've been there, and you'll get through this.

The impact is most powerful in small, very human moments. Like the middle schooler who clutched a stress ball from one of the self-care kits Sarah's team delivered, holding it tightly as if it were the first thing that could quiet the storms inside him. Or the girl in an underfunded school who opened her kit, paused at the sight of the journal, and ran her fingers slowly across its cover as if she had finally been given a safe place to hold her thoughts. These aren't statistics; they're lives softened by kindness, dignity, and the sense that someone out there cares.

Accessibility remains at the heart of Sarah's mission. She knows therapy can be expensive and out of reach, so her nonprofit makes sure resources are free or low-cost. They deliver kits to homeless shelters, schools, and community centers. They raise grants and donations to keep it all going. Every detail is designed with one simple question: *What would have helped my brother?*

Sarah is still a student herself, balancing exams with leading a global nonprofit. Yet she doesn't see her work as extraordinary. To her, it's simply necessary. Because healing doesn't always come in big dramatic moments. Sometimes it starts with a journal, a conversation, or a simple reminder that you are not alone.

What began as one girl's heartbreak has grown into a movement of compassion reaching thousands. Through Mind4Youth, Sarah is honoring her brother's journey while rewriting the way young people see mental health. She has turned her pain into purpose, and in doing so, has given countless others hope that light can be found, even in the darkest places.

(MKRO Kindness Award Winner, Feb 2025)

Reflection: Sarah proves that one person's empathy can ripple outward to touch thousands of lives. What is one tradition of kindness you'd like to pass on to future generations?

Every sunrise is an invitation for us to arise and brighten someone's day.

– Richelle E Goodrich

WIDENING HORIZONS

When Catherine Agarwal walked into her first college biology class in Lubbock, Texas, she couldn't help but think of the kids she had grown up alongside, kids every bit as bright and curious as she was, but without the same chances to discover their love of science. Catherine had been one of the lucky ones. Her school offered a small but powerful STEM (Science, Technology, Engineering, Math) program that gave her a glimpse into the world of discovery: after-school clubs, hands-on projects, and teachers who encouraged her questions. It changed her trajectory. But for so many kids from low-income families like hers, those opportunities simply didn't exist.

But she couldn't shake the thought of all the kids who never had those opportunities. So one day, sitting in biology class while her professor went on about DNA, the actual code of life, she thought, What about the middle schooler who'll never even hold a test tube? Who'll never know how cool it is to pull

DNA out of a strawberry? Who'll never imagine themselves as a doctor or engineer simply because no one had given them the chance. That thought, how much potential was being lost, hit her hard.

Right then, Catherine decided she wasn't going to wait until she was "established" or wore a white coat. She was going to start now.

That decision became Widening Horizons, a student-led program she founded to bring free, hands-on STEM fun to schools that didn't have access to it.

At first, it was just Catherine and four friends lugging boxes of supplies into classrooms, armed with curiosity and determination. They weren't polished teachers, but they knew how to make science come alive. The kids' eyes lit up as they built lava lamps in test tubes, created monsters with genetic traits, and made bath bombs fizz to life.

"You don't need fancy equipment to spark curiosity," Catherine said. "Everyday items can hold the power to change a child's future."

Soon, word spread. More undergraduate students wanted to join, drawn in by Catherine's vision. Within five years, her tiny group of five had become a team of more than thirty volunteers, future doctors, engineers, educators, even artists, who all shared a belief that every child deserves the chance to dream bigger.

Catherine also recognized barriers she herself had once faced. When she discovered a local middle school had an all-boys science club, she immediately partnered with other women at Texas Tech to launch an all-girls STEM program. She wanted young girls to look around the room and see mentors who looked like them, living proof that science wasn't just for the boys.

The pandemic threatened to end everything. Classrooms closed, budgets tightened, and hands-on learning nearly disappeared. But Catherine refused to let those kids be forgotten. She and her team got creative, they built and distributed more than 1,000 science kits, complete with experiments, instructions, and a promise: learning would not be canceled. Over Zoom, volunteers guided kids through the each experiment, laughing, learning, and keeping that spark alive.

Today, Widening Horizons has touched the lives of more than five hundred kids through schools, libraries, and even a local science museum. But for Catherine, the real magic isn't in the awards or recognition, it's in the moments. Like when a kid once whispered, "I'm not good at science" looks up grinning and says, "I want to be an engineer."

Now a medical student in Dallas, Texas, Catherine still carries that same fire. Her dream is to serve her community as a physician and continue mentoring kids from underserved backgrounds, because she knows one simple truth: sometimes, one spark of kindness can open a whole new horizon.

(MKRO Kindness Award Winner, Aug 2025)

Reflection: Catherine reminds us that one spark of opportunity can change a life. Have you ever helped someone who didn't know you were the one helping them? How did that feel?

When you feel lost, treating others as you hope to be treated is true north.

– Carolyn Hax

MATT KURTZ: A LIFE OF QUIET KINDNESS

And at the end of this book, we return to Matt, not in grief, but in gratitude, to honor the life that sparked it all.

A little bit about Matt, the reason we started, Matt's Kindness Ripples On.

Some people shine so brightly in life that even when they're gone, their light lingers, warming hearts, inspiring actions, and reminding us what it means to truly care. Matt Kurtz was one of those people.

While his life ended far too soon, Matt's legacy lives on in the countless lives he touched through his quiet, consistent acts of compassion. He wasn't the kind of person who broadcast his good deeds. In fact, after his passing, story after story came pouring in, tales of kindness Matt never shared, because that's just who he was. His compassion wasn't performative. It was instinctual. It was real.

Matt had a heart of gold, wrapped in a silly, lovable personality. He was goofy and lighthearted, but deeply empathetic. He had a way of seeing people, really seeing them, especially those who were often overlooked. And when he saw someone hurting or in need, he acted. No hesitation. No questions asked. No spotlight needed.

One winter, Matt bought an old van just for a road trip to Vancouver so he and his beloved dog, Tyson, would have a place to sleep without worrying about dog-friendly hotels. Most people would've sold the van afterward. Not Matt. On his return, he gave the van to a homeless person so they'd have a warm place to sleep. No paperwork. No expectations. Just love.

Another time, while walking home after playing basketball, Matt noticed a homeless man without shoes. Without a second thought, he took off his own and handed them over. He walked the rest of the way home barefoot. Again, that was just Matt.

It wasn't unusual for him to quietly reach into his pocket and hand over bills to someone in need. He never looked for thanks. He just believed that if he could help someone, he should. One friend recalled Matt telling them, "Don't worry about paying him back, just pay it forward. Always help others."

And help others, he did.

Matt's kindness left an unforgettable imprint on those lucky enough to know him. A few of his friends shared what he meant to them.

Shane said, "I envied his capacity for optimism and empathy. There's no doubt I'm a better person because of him."

Abby remembered Matt as someone who "never had a negative word to say" and showed her "tremendous kindness during the hardest years" of her life.

Claudio shared that Matt supported him when even his own family had walked away. Matt helped him buy work clothes, pay rent, and bring his kids home. "Your son helped me prosper in life and become who I am today," he said.

Spencer said, "Matt was the most accepting, genuine person I've ever met. He changed my life. Truly."

And Ricky remembered Matt as "one of the nicest people I've ever met. He was there for me at one of my lowest points. Always supportive. Always kind."

Matt's life was a testament to the power of small, meaningful actions. He believed that kindness, even in its simplest form, could make a lasting difference. And he was right.

For those who knew Matt, and even those learning about him now, his message is clear: Kindness doesn't need a reason. It doesn't need recognition. It just needs a willing heart.

So today, we invite you to do something kind, something small, quiet, and full of love. And when you do, think of Matt Kurtz.

Because the ripple of his kindness still moves through the world.

And it always will.

Reflection: Matt didn't wait for the right moment to be kind; he acted from the heart, quietly and selflessly, every chance he got. When was the last time you helped someone without expecting anything in return, and how can you make that kind of kindness a part of your everyday life?

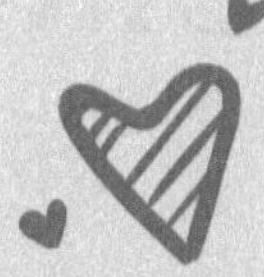

No matter what happens in life, be good to people. Being good to people is a wonderful legacy to leave behind.

– Taylor Swift

KEEP THE KINDNESS GOING

While you've reached the last page of this book, the kindness doesn't stop here.

At Matts Kindness Ripples On, https://mattskindnessrippleson.com/ we continue to celebrate extraordinary people who make kindness a way of life. We've awarded over $20,000 in kindness grants and awards so far, and thanks to the proceeds from this book, we're just getting started.

Join us as we keep the ripples going.

1. **Kindness Giveaway**

   Sign up for our blog and receive a dose of kindness delivered to your inbox (only two emails a month), filled with inspiring stories, uplifting messages, and real-life examples of kindness in action.

   As a thank you, each month we randomly select five new subscribers to receive our exclusive sticker: *"Whatever you do today, do it with kindness."* Sign up today for your chance to win!

   (Sign up on the MKRO home page, **MattsKindnessRipplesOn.com** https://mattskindness-rippleson.com/ "Subscribe to our Blog")

2. **Spread Kindness Right Now**

Leave a quick review of this book on Amazon or Goodreads. Reviews are one of the most powerful ways to keep the ripple of kindness growing. The more people discover this book, the more proceeds we get to help us fund even more kindness grants and awards, giving future Kindness Heroes the resources they need to spread compassion where it's needed most. Thank you in advance, it truly means so much.

3. **Nominate a Kindness Hero**

Know someone who leads with love and makes a difference? Nominate them for our Kindness Award, winners receive a certificate of appreciation and $250 to recognize their impact.
At **MattsKindnessRipplesOn.com** https://mattskindnessrippleson.com/get-involved/nominate-someone/

4. **Apply for a Kindness Grant**

We offer $500 grants to help bring your compassionate ideas to life. Submit your request and let's make something beautiful happen together. At **MattsKindnessRipplesOn. com** https://mattskindnessrippleson.com/get-involved/submit-ideas-grant/

5. **Follow, Share, and Tag** @MattsKindnessRipplesOn

6. **Welcome to Our Community of Kindness**
We're so glad you found us. This is just the beginning.

Questions or comments, email me at:
MattsKindnessRipplesOn@gmail.com

MEET THE KINDNESS HEROES

These are the extraordinary individuals whose stories are shared in this book. Each of them saw a need, chose compassion, and created ripples of kindness that continue to spread far beyond their own communities.

Aanand Mehta – *Phoenix, AZ* ----------------------------------- *196*

Wheels of Joy, (Magical Motors: https://magicalmotors.org)

Adam Rosante – *Amagansett, NY* ----------------------------------- *155*

Kindness, Lived Daily, (Good Eats: https://www.goodeatsprogram.org/, Homekeeper: https://homekeeperprogram.org/)

Agha Haider – *Ballwin, MO* ---*82*

Spreading Literacy and Joy, (Literacy Initiative: http://www.literacy-initiative.org)

Amanda Durante – *Bridgewater, MA* ----------------------- *228*

Carrying Love, Not Trash Bags, (Wandering Hearts Project: https://www.wanderingheartproject.org/)

Ashley Beeler – *Bloomington, IN* ---*42*

Filling the Gap, (Little Free Pantry: https://lfpbloomington.org)

Barbara Buckley – *Abington, MA* ---*22*

The Everlasting Hug, (Annie's Kindness Blankets: https://annieskind-nessblankets.org/)

Carmen Garner – *Upper Marlboro, MD*-------------------------------*102*

Casting Hope

Catherine Agarwal – *Richardson, TX*-------------------------------*252*

Widening Horizons

Chelsea Phaire – *New Fairfield, CT*-------------------------------*66*

Coloring Outside the Lines, (Chelsea's Charity: https://www.chel-seascharity.org)

Colby Phillips – *Berlin, MD*------------------------------- *151*

A Life of Kindness

Connie Hammes – *Lake Park, MN*-------------------------------*54*

Catio Magic, (The Marshmallow Foundation: https://www.marshmal-lowfoundation.org)

Curtis Jones – **Longmont, CO**-------------------------------*236*

The Mad Hatter Project, (Mt Sanitas Mad Hatter Project: https://www.facebook.com/MtSanitasMadHatterProject)

Dustin Beeler – *Bloomington, IN* -------------------------------*42*

Filling the Gap, (Little Free Pantry: https://lfpbloomington.org)

Elaine Mack – *Mesa, AZ*------------------------------- *224*

Champions for Seniors

Franziska Trautmann – *New Orleans, LA*------------------------------70

From Wine Night to Wetlands, (Glass Half Full: https://glasshalffull. co/)

George Ahearn – *Woodinville, WA*----------------------------- 26

From Waste to Hope, (East West Food Rescue: https://www. eastwestfoodrescue.org/)

Hannah Blackwell – *Chicago, IL*----------------------------------216

Planting Hope, (Southside Blooms: https://www.southsideblooms.com/)

Holly Christensen – *Palmer, AK*--------------------------------------10

Weaving Joy, (The Magic Yarn Project https://themagicyarnproject. com/)

Humza Zaida – *Avon, CT*--110

From Hunger to Hope

Jackie Atkins – *Long Branch, NJ*------------------------------------232

Fighting for Their Future, (NJ Give a Kid a Dream: https://njgakad. com/)

Jamie Wallace-Griner – *Austin, TX*--------------------------------18

A Sanctuary Built by Love, (Safe In Austin: https://www.safeinaustin. org)

Jason Long – *Berlin, MD*--172

Sheltering with Compassion, (OC Cold Weather Shelter: https://www. facebook.com/ocmdCOLD/)

Jayde Powell – *Las Vegas, NV*---62

Shopping Angels, (Shopping Angels: https://shoppingangelsglobal.org/)

Jennie Bouchard-Young – *Wilton, ME*------------------------------244

A Life Woven with Kindness and Purpose

Jerry Martin – *Mesa, AZ*---224

Champions for Seniors

Jessica Munoz – *Waialua, HI*--50

From ER to Empowerment, (Hoʻōla Nā Pua: https://hoolanapua.org, Pearl Haven: https://pearlhavenhawaii.org/)

Jessica Ong – *San Diego, CA*---38

A Chapter of Kindness

Jude Al-Hamad – *Berlin, MD*-------------------------------------204

Kindness in Every Basket

Kaig Lightner – *Portland, OR*-------------------------------------208

Creating Belonging Through Soccer, (Portland Community Football Club: https://www.pcfc.co/)

Kristen Weinberg – *Sandy Spring, MD*--------------------------131

What's Your 50? (What's Your 50? https://www.facebook.com/ Whatsyour50donation)

Larry Abrams – *Pennsauken, NJ*--------------------------------- 176

Turning Pages, Changing Lives, (Book Smiles: https://www.booksmiles. org/)

Linda McGean – *Berlin, MD*--------------------------------------240

Leading with Heart

Liz Buechele – *New York, NY*------------------------------------122

The Road to Kindness, (The Smile Project: https://www.the-smile-project.com)

Marina Arias – *McKinleyville, CA* ----------------------------86

Kindness in Motion

Max Steitz – *New Orleans, LA*----------------------------------70

From Wine Night to Wetlands, (Glass Half Full: https://glasshalffull. co/)

Mike Fahey – *Selkirk, NY*---------------------------------------46

Serving Up Hope, (Street Soldiers: https://streetsoldierscommunity. wordpress.com)

Mike Goldberg – *Islamorada, FL*--------------------------------98

From Wall Street to the Ocean Floor, (I.CARE: https://icareaboutcoral. org/)

Mindy Oursley – *Canton, OH*-----------------------------------34

Changing Young Lives

Muhammad Abdul-Hadi – *Philadelphia, PA*---------------------30

Serving Second Chances, (Down North Pizza: https://www.downnorthpizza.com/ Down North Foundation: https://www.downnorthfoundation.org/)

Neel Sood – Bridgewater, NJ-------------------------------------- 220

Hearts of Kindness

Nicole Munoz – Pacific Grove, CA-------------------------------------94

Embracing Identity

Nigel Mushambi – Missouri City, TX--------------------------------90

Baking a Better World

Quilen Blackwell – Chicago, IL-------------------------------------216

Planting Hope, (Southside Blooms: https://www.southsideblooms.com/)

Rachael Rosenberg – Woodland Hills, CA--------------------------164

A Bundle of Compassion, (Bundles of Kindness: https://bundlesofkind-ness.org/)

Randal Wyatt – Portland, OR--------------------------------------- 135

Taking Ownership, (Taking Ownership PDX: https://takingownership-pdx.org/)

Rena Rosen – Chicago, IL---184

Warm Hands, Warm Hearts, (Knit for a Unique Fit: https://www.facebook.com/groups/968877786968046)

Renee Fahey – Selkirk, NY--------------------------------------- 46

Serving Up Hope, (Street Soldiers: https://streetsoldierscommunity.wordpress.com)

Rhiannon Menn – Kihei, HI-------------------------------------192

Serving Kindness, One Meal at a Time, (Lasagna Love: https://app.lasagnaloveportal.org/)

Robert Peterpaul – *Norwalk, CT*---*212*

Spreading Smiles One Episode at a Time, (Thomas Peterpaul Foundation: https://www.thomaspeterpaul.org/, The Art of Kindness Podcast: https://open.spotify.com/show/32Rm1xYVdxZIQNk8avyFwY)

Ronald Braunstein – *Melrose, MA*----------------------------------- *188*

Changing Minds Through Music, (Me 2 Orchestra: https://me2music.org/)

Ruby Chitsey – *Harrison, AR*---*180*

The Power of Small Wishes, (Three Wishes for Ruby's Residents: https://3wishesproject.org)

Sarah Goody – *Corte Madera, CA*--------------------------------------*106*

A Voice for the Planet, (Climate Now: https://www.climatenow.solutions/)

Sarah Shelke – *Cupertino, CA*---*248*

Light in Dark Places, (Mind 4 Youth: https://mind4youth.com/)

Shia Mankin – *California City, CA*---------------------------*114, 117*

Eighteen Acts, Endless Impact

And Then Came the Ripples

Shirley Raines – *Long Beach, CA*--*74*

Beauty with Purpose, (Beauty 2 The Streetz: https://www.beauty2thestreetz.org/)

Shreyaa Venkat – *Ashburn, VA*---*58*

Where Kindness Begins, (NEST4US: https://nest4us.org/)

Silas Scauzillo – *Rockledge, FL*--------------------------------------*147*

The Kindness Ambassador

Simon Emmanuel Mollel – *Arusha, Tanzania*------------------*200*

Restoring Women's Voices, (Nadumu Masaii's Women's Organization: https://nmwtz.org/)

Sonia Su – *Clarksville, MD*---*78*

From Patient to Provider, (Kits to Heart: https://kitstoheart.org/)

Sriya Tallapragada – *New Providence, NJ*-------------------------*127*

From Isolation to Inclusion, (Girls Who STEAM: https://girlswhosteam. org)

Stephen Knight – *Richardson, TX*-----------------------------------*14*

Second Chances, (Dogs Matter: https://www.dogsmatter2.org/)

Stephen Schirra – *Ellington, CT*-------------------------------------*143*

Hope Takes the Field, (Around the Worlds: https://aroundtheworlds. org/)

Susan Melton – *Cheboygan, MI*-------------------------------------*168*

Sidewalks of Hope, (Sidewalk Chalk Project: https://www.facebook. com/SidewalkChalkProject)

Taha Umar – *Holmdel, NJ*---*160*

Bridging Borders with Compassion

Trisha Long – *Berlin, MD*--*172*

Sheltering with Compassion, (OC Cold Weather Shelter: https://www. facebook.com/ocmdCOLD/)

Valerianne Hinkley – *Farmington, ME*-----------------------------*139*

When Kindness Fights Back

ABOUT THE AUTHOR

Jackie Kurtz lives on the Eastern Shore of Maryland with her husband, Ron. Together, they enjoy an active life filled with pickleball, boating, biking, reading, and time spent in nature. Traveling is a favorite joy, especially trips to Boulder, Colorado, where they visit their son, Brian.

For Jackie, nature is more than a place, it's a sacred space where she feels deeply connected to the universe and to her beloved son, Matt, who passed away in 2017. His spirit continues to inspire her every day.

Jackie feels incredibly grateful for the love and laughter she shares with her close-knit circle of friends and family. Their kindness and connection fuel her passion for telling stories that uplift, inspire, and remind us of the everyday heroes who make the world a better place.

MattsKindnessRipplesOn.com
https://mattskindnessrippleson.com/

@MattsKindness (Instagram)
https://www.instagram.com/mattskindness/

MattsKindnessRipplesOn (Facebook)
https://www.facebook.com/mattskindnessrippleson

ACKNOWLEDGEMENTS

From the bottom of my heart, I am so deeply grateful to all of the Kindness Heroes featured in this book.

This collection wouldn't exist without the remarkable people whose stories you've just read, individuals who remind us, in the most powerful ways, that kindness isn't just a feeling, it's a choice, a commitment, and sometimes, an act of extraordinary courage.

To each of them: thank you for showing us what compassion, resilience, and humanity look like in action. Your stories are the heartbeat of this book, and your impact will ripple far beyond these pages.

And to you, the reader: thank you for picking up this book. The fact that you're holding it in your hands tells us you care about kindness, too, and that makes you part of this growing ripple.

I hope these stories have shifted how you see "heroes." That they've shown you that kindness is not small or ordinary, it's powerful. It changes lives. And now, it's your turn. Go spread kindness in whatever way feels right for you.

To my incredible kindness community, thank you for believing in the mission of Matt's Kindness Ripples On. Whether you've followed along, shared our stories, donated, nominated someone, or applied for a grant, your support fuels every ripple we send out into the world. I'm endlessly grateful for every one of you.

To my editor, Tarah Threadgill, thank you for your efficiency, insight, and thoughtful recommendations, which greatly improved Kindness Heroes. I sincerely appreciate your expertise and support.

To the incredible women in my life. I'm so deeply grateful for your friendship and love. I am so lucky to have you in my life.

Some of you I've known since childhood, Sarah and my SOS girls: Merv, Linda, Connie, and Lynne (and Karen and Jeanne, who are surely causing trouble in heaven). You know all my secrets, and every embarrassing story. We've shared a lifetime of laughter and so many memories that still make me smile out loud. Whenever one of us had a bad idea, the rest of us were always *all in*. Let's keep the laughter, and the bad ideas, flowing.

To my friend Karen, whom I met when we were both planning our weddings. I'm sure she is exploring heaven with the same spirit she explored life.

Some friendships came through our children, like my friend Janet and my wonderful Gourmet Group: Mara, Bonnie, Donna, and Susan. Thank you for the connection, community, love, and great food. And thank you for bringing all the gourmet food to my house when it was my turn, you could count on me for wine and salad.

Some of you I met through work, my amazing Luxmanor crew: Louise, Sharon, and Gloria, what a gift your friendship has been.

And then, there's my Pickleball tribe I found after retiring, Leslie, Lynne, Claire, Linda, Kelly, and Susie, you've added fun, energy, and camaraderie to this chapter of life, and I'm so glad we found each other on the courts.

To Nini (and Pop Pop), thank you for being such wonderful grandparents to Matt and Brian. I could always count on you to help out when needed.

To my brother Mike, thank you for taking the role of "big brother" seriously. I couldn't have picked a better brother. I love you.

To my mom and favorite travel companion, thank you for the many unforgettable adventures we've shared. So many countries, so many stories, and so much laughter. And thank you for showing me (with a healthy dose of humor) all the things I have to look forward to as I get older.

To my fabulous nieces and nephews, and the great ones too: Connor, Jessie, Dana, Orlando, Rosie, and Eli, you light up my life with your love, energy, and joy. I love watching you grow and thrive.

To Brian, thank you for the challenges you gave me when you were growing up (I hope I rose to the occasion!). And thank you for the love, support, and laughter you've brought into my life ever since. I admire your generous heart, your fun-loving spirit, and your one-liners that always make me laugh. Thank you for letting me give advice without too many eye rolls. I love you with all my heart.

And finally, to my husband, Ron, thank you for always taking care of our family, for making sure we're safe, loved, and laughing. Thank you for all the memories we've made and for sticking with me through every twist and turn. I'm grateful to have you by my side, in good times, in tough times, and through all the crazy in between. You know how much I love you, even when you're trying to tell me I'm wrong, but I'm not :)